A Small Cup of Light

This is a praiseful realization:
love is bit and bridle, despair, the beast.
To live well is to learn how to ride,
how to lean into grief.

Ben Palpant

Praise For
A Small Cup of Light

"Ben Palpant tells his story so very well, weaving past and present, imagination and experience into an amazing tapestry. I was quite taken with it. Honestly, a stunning book. It reminds me of Simone Weil's essay on affliction. Ben has done what few authors do. He has written a book about his own experience of suffering, which was mysterious and tumultuous. Yet he told his story so transparently and effortlessly that I gazed through his story to think about my story and the human story. He also wrote with elegance and grace. It is a superb book in every way."

–Gerald Sittser, professor of Theology at Whitworth University and author of *A Grace Disguised* and *A Grace Revealed*

"Ben Palpant is a fellow traveler on the journey through pain and adversity. As such, he knows there are no easy answers or quick fixes when we encounter hardships and heartaches in our lives. With grace and compassion, Ben encourages readers to seek God's presence, even when He seems absent, and pursue transformation, even when it seems impossible. Ben's book arrived in my hands at a time when my well-constructed world was slowly being dismantled. His words, full of warmth and wisdom, provided genuine comfort while challenging me to look squarely at painful issues I'd prefer to avoid. Ben speaks from the heart–and his hard-won insights touched my own. I have read each page slowly and intentionally, and I have been ministered to by Ben's insights, sensitivity, openness, and artistry. Already his book is having a profound influence... certainly on me."

–Keith Wall, coauthor of *Heaven and the Afterlife* and *Real Life, Real Miracles*

"In a gorgeous and tender, beautiful and graceful clarion call to the heart of our despair and the fierceness of our inner desolations, Ben Palpant draws us to an intimate encounter with the God of all consolation. He courageously broaches the inner life of weakness and the sorrows we harbor. *A Small Cup of Light* is the sustenance we need to pass through the valley of the shadow and arrive on the other side more whole, more humble, and more alive."

–Shann Ray Ferch, author of *American Masculine* and *Balefire: Poems.*

"Adversity, sorrow, disappointment. None of us ever want it. But all of us will surely face it. And when we do, we are invariably surprised, unprepared. Ben Palpant's beautiful book–beautifully conceived and beautifully written–explores the dark profiles of suffering with the glistening light of hope. Reading *A Small Cup of Light* powerfully moved me, not only by reminding me of God's good providence, but also by provoking in me memories of all the ways His providence has sustained me through my own days of bewildering adversities. By all means, *tolle lege*, take and read."

–George Grant, pastor, author, and renowned speaker

"Ben Palpant's *A Small Cup of Light* caused me to weep for joy, opened my mind to dream of future glory, and engaged my heart with gripping stories of personal, searing truth. In these pages, you will find a faithful and honest pilgrim who invites you through deep valleys of pain to illuminate your own mysterious journey with God in surprising joy. If you are like me, you too will find your soul in celebration."

–Dave Hutchins, author of *Courageous Parenting: the passionate pursuit of your teen's heart*

A SMALL CUP OF LIGHT

a drink in the desert

Ben Palpant

To Kristen
my favorite poem

Let me find Thy light in my darkness,
Thy life in my death,
Thy joy in my sorrow,
Thy grace in my sin,
Thy riches in my poverty,
Thy glory in my valley.

—from *The Valley of Vision:*
A collection of Puritan Prayers & Devotions

But tomorrow, dawn will come the way I picture her,
barefoot and disheveled, standing outside my window
in one of the fragile cotton dresses of the poor.
She will look in at me with her thin arms extended,
offering a handful of birdsong and a small cup of light.

—Billy Collins, from "Tuesday, June 4, 1991"

Contents

A Note To The Reader

This book chronicles a two year physical, mental, and spiritual crisis, the effects of which I still carry with me. In a matter
of a few weeks, I was reduced to an infant–learning again
to read and walk and feed myself. The unnamed illness that
hamstrung my hopes made itself at home in my body nearly
overnight, rerouting the wiring of my mind. Bedridden and
bewildered, I began sorting through my little red wagon of existential questions: Who am I? What does God want of me? Is
he really in charge? With normality unraveling and my identity
lost, I eventually floundered in despair.

It seemed fair at the time, and it seems fair even now,
to ask whether suffering is a valuable part of life. Suffering
exists in varying degrees, of course, and arises from innumerable causes. You might have cancer or face unemployment. You

might still be recovering from the devastation of a failed marriage or have had a child walk away from all your convictions. You may be the victim of violence. Perhaps you live day to day, one breath at time, with loss: a miscarriage, a spouse's death, a health failure.

This book is my attempt to re-enter one of the darkest seasons of my life and come to terms with the mystery, brokenness, and hope that I encountered in the wilderness. Perhaps you, too, are wandering through a wilderness in life. Perhaps you are looking for answers to the same questions. I don't know your story, but I know my own. I invite you into mine in hopes that by reading it, you will better see your own story. Maybe together we will discover what God led us into this wilderness to find: himself.

*"I have a feeling that my boat
has struck, down there in the depths,
against a great thing."*

Juan Ramon Jimenez
from "Oceans"

CHAPTER 1

My Unmaking

I used to think there were only two ways to meet my Maker: a blow to the head or a free ride on Elijah's flaming chariot. Either I would kick the bucket or experience a miraculous quantum transport—that simple. Two months after my thirty-third birthday, I discovered another way to encounter God: the agony of affliction.

That afternoon I woke from a nap with my brain on fire, like hot coals pressed in the grey matter. The vicious pain induced me to crawl outside and burrow my head into a wind-swept snow bank just to stay alive. My four-year-old son found me. He stood, stocky and objectively curious, as is his way, observing my strange new behavior.

"Get Mom," I whispered.

I wanted someone to reach inside my brain and lift out the coals. My wife was the closest help, but that's not why I sent my son away. The truth is that I did not want my little boy to see me in such a pathetic and vulnerable state. Despite all the pain, I cared only to save face, to dispel the imprint of my frailty on my son's psyche.

A phone call dispelled the fear of an aneurysm, and my wife cooled the heat in my head, calming me down enough so that I slept, though fitfully. I woke in the middle of the night with my brain racing. My mind leapt from one disconnected idea to another with growing appetite, absent was any sign of the lingering thickness and throb that usually followed migraine headaches. It felt like my mind sat in front of a screen that flashed thirty bizarre images every second but could not keep up with them.

The speed exhilarated and terrified me. I tried to move my arm, but my too busy mind could not send the command. Only with great force of will could I move my body, every movement in slow motion. It took me nearly an hour to henpeck an email to my boss informing him that I could not go to work the next day. I wrote only two short sentences.

Three days later, I sluggishly returned to my work as a teacher. I pretended like everything was back to normal, but it wasn't. Termites were eating at my house of confidence which finally collapsed one week later.

I was working through *The Imitation of Christ* with my students one morning when it happened. Reading aloud a chapter as they followed along, I suddenly saw a word that I did not understand. I kept reading, but one minute later I read another unintelligible word. Thirty seconds later, another. This time the word was short, an everyday word that I knew I should comprehend. Twenty seconds, another one. Ten seconds, yet another. And then my eyes scanned not just words, but sentences that I could not understand. Those sentences formed entire paragraphs that were lost on me. I felt the house falling around me and panicked inside.

I stopped reading, quietly asked a student to continue, and left the room. I did not know what was happening and I did not know what to do, but I knew I wanted no one to witness it. So I staggered toward the locker rooms, feeling the strength slowly seep from not only my mind, but also my arms and legs.

Fortunately, a colleague saw me and asked if I was alright. I lied, of course, and tried to throw him off the scent, but he knew me too well and followed at a distance. When I found a chair and started weeping in fear, he turned the corner and pulled up a chair in front of me.

"What's happening, Ben?" he asked quietly.

"I don't know," I said. "I'm confused."

He laid his hands on me and prayed for me on the spot before getting help. I've wondered since why he chose to pray before getting help, but I'm thankful that he did. His prayer slowed my panic. A few minutes later, my boss drove me home.

The road home climbed through the hills and leveled out amongst farmland, now blanketed by snow. I pressed my face against the window to rest and stare at the passing frozen landscape. We talked some, most of which I don't remember, but I remember that he encouraged me not to worry. My classes would be covered, and I could take my time. Fatigue set in quickly and I had no strength to worry. He helped me into the house where I collapsed on the couch.

When I awoke, many hours later, shadows filled the room. My wife had left to pick up the kids from their various afternoon activities, and I should have been alone in the house, but I wasn't. I felt someone in the room with me. When I stirred, he spoke.

"Hello, Son." My father's voice was a quiet comfort.

"Hello, Dad."

We sat quietly while my mind crawled back one week to January 10th, the day before my mind had caught fire. That Saturday, we were celebrating one of my children's birthdays. Dad had pulled up a chair and asked, "How are you, Son?"

"I'm tired," I admitted. "You know, we got home last night at 1:00 a.m. but the basketball team won the big game in overtime. We're still undefeated. And my work at church is pretty busy, but going well."

"How's school?" he asked.

"Teaching is teaching, a lot of hard work, but classes are good over all. I can't complain."

"And the kids?"

"Well, parenting's a blast. They keep us hopping."

"How are you sleeping?"

Unprepared for this question, I blurted out, "Honestly, I don't sleep great. I'm usually tired, but I can sometimes snag a few minutes of sleep during lunch break. I sneak into my truck and doze. But, you know, sleep is overrated. I can sleep when I'm dead."

He chuckled, sort of. "Son, I don't like the pace you're living and I'm afraid it might catch up to you. Your body needs sleep. God made it that way. I've seen the ill-effects of sleep-lessness in my hospital patients and I've experienced them myself. I appreciate all the good things you're doing, but you might want to slow down just a bit."

He was genuinely concerned, as father and physician, and I tried to be genuine in response. "Alright, Dad, I'll try." But I had no intention of trying. I brushed him off.

The next day I buried my head in the snow. And here he was, a week later, sitting in the darkness with me. Quiet. No condemnation. Just loud enough to let me know that he was there. The thought crossed my mind that he should be treating patients at the hospital, since he was a physician, and not sitting with me.

"Why are you here?" I whispered.

"Oh, I left the hospital early as soon as I heard. Thought I'd check on you."

He didn't stay long. I had no physical strength and mental fatigue prevented conversation, but he didn't see any cause for panic. He offered names of medical specialists whom I should visit in case the confusion continued, gave me a hug, and encouraged me not to worry.

Not worry? That's what my boss had said, too. But I felt plenty worried.

I did not improve. Over the next week I visited specialists and took their prescriptions. The neurologist made me stand on one foot and tap my head, dancing to the halting beat of the checklist on his clipboard. Apparently I danced well enough to require no further tests, no clicking machines. After all the M.D.'s and Ph.D's had cleared me without a definitive diagnosis, I visited the guy who was a last gasp, a guy reputed to stick "closer to the earth."

He asked me if I had spit at any point in my life. I told him that, yes, sometimes I hocked a good one to see if I could hit a tree in mid-stride from ten feet. In fact, if I could boast for a moment...

"You might reconsider such, shall we say, activities."

"What does spitting have to do with my fatigue and confusion?"

"Well, I'm not sure, but I know that every time a human person spits, he loses a part of him that will not return."

I felt a deep urge to tell him the situation could be more dire than I had first admitted: I also enjoyed rolling down the car window, checking behind and in front, measuring the wind and speed, and seeing if I could hit a rock or a pole on the other side of the road—while driving—but decided against it. Someday, when I'm finally face to face with my Savior, he'll probably say, "Remember that doc you flippantly dismissed? He was right." I'll probably mumble something about trying to spit when nobody was looking and shuffle my feet.

"Thank you...sir." I was going to say, "Doctor," but it didn't seem appropriate.

All these good people tried their best to solve me, prescribing solutions for the headaches and fatigue, but they were unable to help where I needed it most: repairing the disintegration of my mind.

We grew weary of sitting in waiting rooms, my wife and I, waiting to recount (again) the series of events that turned my mind into a one-legged beggar trying to scrape together a living.

One by one, the medical community shook their collective heads and could only offer theories. How quickly one can reach the limits of our medical knowledge. What I wanted most of all, and what they couldn't deliver, was a name for my illness. I desperately wanted something to fight by name. Call it "termites". Call it "dry rot". I didn't really care, but I wanted to call it something.

When we weren't in a doctor's office, I rested on the couch trying to do mental push-ups. My mind had difficulty with simple lines of thought and with simple words. I had no strength in my legs and just enough strength in my hands to hold a book for a few minutes. I could not read much, mostly I read children's books, the kinds with big pictures and short words. Still, they were hard enough. A stack of them leaned against the couch, always next to me, a stack that I hid whenever friends came to check in or bring a meal.

My embarrassment ran deep. My twelve year teaching career, my identity as father and husband; my life as I had formerly known it, were in serious jeopardy. I wanted my body back. I wanted my mind back. I wanted my life.

I lay curled in a fetal position one night, listening to my wife's voice. In the evenings, she just talked, speaking light into my darkness by reading verses to me. I needed a touchstone and she knew it, so she kept gently pointing toward

Christ. She set aside her fears to speak into my own.

As she spoke, I remembered another woman's voice from many years earlier. My mother used to speak truth into my ears, even jotting down verses on paper and taping them above my headboard during my tumultuous nightmare seasons. I suffered from paralyzing night-terrors, and she would sit on the edge of my bed and read the Psalms.

"May the Lord answer you in the hour of trouble!
The name of the God of Jacob be your strong tower. May He give you help from the sanctuary and send you aid from Zion!"[1]

"God is our shelter and our refuge,
a timely help in trouble;
so we are not afraid when the earth heaves
and the mountains are hurled into the sea,
when its waters seethe in tumult..."[2]

"Be gracious to me, O God, be gracious;
for I have made thee my refuge.
I will take refuge in the shadow of thy wings

---

1   Psalm 20 NEBV
2   Psalm 46 NEBV

until the storms are past"[3]

But even as my wife whispered reality into my ears, and although I remembered the reorienting whispers of my youth, I felt myself sinking into a bog. Like finding my feet stuck in mud with cold water sloshing around my knees and looking around at a marshland stretching out as far as I could see. Worse yet, like knowing that night was falling with all the stars veiled and my flashlight quickly dimming.

Light. I needed light.

"Pilot me, O precious Christ!" my soul cried.

I seemed to hear him reply in the distance, "I am, my child, just as I always have."

"Where you go, I cannot follow!" I cried.

"Fear not," he said. "I am carrying you into the darkness."

And I was frightened.

_____

3   Psalm 57 NEBV

A Small Cup of Light

"So short a time
To teach my life its transposition to
This difficult and unaccustomed key!"

Edna St. Vincent Millay
from "Interim"

CHAPTER 2

Born To Trouble and Blindness

"Affliction is a treasure, and scarce any man hath enough of it."[1]

So wrote John Donne.

I suppose he should have known. After sending five of his children and his wife into eternity and suffering under the wrack of stomach cancer, he preached his own funeral and posed in a death shroud for his final painting. I imagine him as the legend describes, wrapped in a sheet while the painter pretended the poet was dead and waited for him to stop itching. If Death had strode through the dog-violets and peeked in at the window just then, he might have laughed outright to see Donne placidly posing.

Affliction is a treasure, he claimed.

He should know. But still. No child in the history of mankind, when asked what he would like to do when he grows up, has ever responded, "I want to suffer."

---

1   John Donne, "Meditation XVII"

I, for one, did not.

I take it upon reliable testimony that I was born on the 23rd of November, in the year of our Lord, 1974. No historians took note. My birth remains superseded on that year's wall of fame by more notable events like Richard Nixon's resignation, the invention of the Rubik's Cube, the night when news anchor Christine Chubbuck put a bullet in her brain on live television, and of course, the premier of Dr. Who. They say that amongst my infant companions were an Irish Setter, a horned toad, and a backyard of dirt.

Born in the Arizona desert, beneath the shadow of the Santa Catalina mountains, I spent the first five years of my life like the four-legged critters of that arid landscape, shyly. Or so they say. I have almost no recollection, only scattered film clippings in the pocket of my memory—a bunk bed, a tire swing, a tile floor, and then there's the short film of my dad teaching me to tie my shoes by the front door.

Some people say the first five years are the most foundational, setting the grooves of one's habits and grinding the lens of one's imagination. What a pity, then, that I have no recollection worth boasting about from those most influential years.

Without my knowledge, God started crafting the poem of my life in those early days. That poem took an unexpected twist when my dad accepted a medical missionary post oversees. At the age of five, my family pulled up roots and re-planted ourselves in Kenya, Africa.

Located at the base of Mt. Elgon, the rural hospital where my father served the medical needs of the local people offered a view wide as the sky above. I could scamper a few houses down and gaze over an enormous valley that spread its agrarian patchwork quilt towards the distant Ugandan border.

My imagination ripened in tropical climes so remote that even seeing airplanes cross the pale heavens in that part of the world was a rare and distant event. I used to scramble up the guava tree and onto the tin roof of our house at the slightest sound of an airplane: a sound as thin and far off as an extended exhale of breath from pursed lips. I would lie down on my back and search the azure sky, learning early to look well past the sound itself for any shimmer of light, usually microscopic, that might betray the gravity-defying object hurtling through the heavens.

Speed intoxicated me. Unfortunately, my father's blue Ford Escort and the hospital's ambulance, a Land Rover, never even threatened to break forty miles per hour. So my friends and I experienced speed vicariously: race cars.

Officially, the Safari Rally covered 2,550 miles of unpaved East African roads in one weekend. Unofficially, it was a nirvana greater than anything else on the earth for fans like me. The route climbed in and out of the Great Rift Valley, and drivers faced unpredictable conditions because of sudden weather and terrain changes.

Of one hundred entrants, fewer than twenty usually finished the race. For my friends and me, the vehicles splashed with dried mud and emblazoned with a thousand bright decals were chariots for the gods and each driver worth deifying. Inside a photo album, I neatly pasted all my collected bubblegum wrappers with drawings of the famous rally cars. We begged, borrowed, or stole—emptying the piggy-bank if necessary—to get another gum wrapper. The gum offered nothing more than a minute of sweetness and three minutes of chewability, but the pictures were priceless because they were the closest we would ever get to real happiness. Or so we thought.

Then one day, for reasons still inexplicable, Dad drove us out into the hinterlands where we flocked roadside with a few hundred other race enthusiasts. Standing in the tall weeds and huddled beneath the spreading eucalyptus trees, we waited to hear the distant whine of strained engines for what seemed like hours.

While the restless crowd waited, one particular goat decided to take a brief nap. It staggered across the dirt road like a drunk and then, as though utterly exhausted, it settled down for a long rest right in the middle of the road. The boys found the goat amusing, but one conscientious man tried fervently to coax it off the road.

Pushing and prodding did no good. He finally reverted to beating its backside with a stick. The goat remained determinedly planted. The man's useless efforts became a kind of diversion for the rest of us until a dread stirred the crowd. The distant roar of engines carried over the plains. I realized, probably much later than the rest, that the goat would soon be at the center of an epic collision.

The goat had no idea of the impending doom, of course, and remained fixed. I joined the crowd in shouting at the goat. Several men battled to get it out of the way. Perhaps growing tired of the abuse or the unwanted attention, it finally rose unsteadily and staggered to the other side of the road before any of the rally cars skidded into sight.

When they finally hurtled around the corner, one car every twenty minutes or so, I had ten seconds to glimpse their mud speckled bodies, the decals, the mounted fog lights, and the two drivers leaning into the curve.

Those cars were everything I had dreamed but the picture of that goat has remained with me all these years as an illustration of naivety and belligerent blindness. He was cluelessly self-assured. Like that goat, I nurtured an unwarranted confidence for a long time. For much of my life, I woke up every morning wearing the same imaginative lens. One colored by false confidence. Failure was for other people and weakness to be avoided completely.

Though I claimed Christ as Lord and I knew that his power is "made perfect in weakness,"[2] I feared weakness more than almost anything else. I convinced myself that I could avoid weakness. I manufactured a thousand excuses for this misconception, of course, but none of them removed the final fact that much of what I assumed in life as reliable was not, in fact, reality.

I was the goat whose confidence was built on a misconception. Until that moment in my classroom, when the words on the page lost their meaning in mass, I was self-reliant. I believed that if I were sufficiently strong enough, good enough, and smart enough, then I could overcome any obstacle. My zeal effectively held weakness at bay until weakness slipped through the back door and crawled through my mind's web of neurons, cutting the power. I felt the suburbs of my mind go dark right in front of my students that January day and I was terrified.

---

2   2 Corinthians 12:9

***

One week after my first mental collapse in the classroom, one week spent denying the reality of my situation, I
tried returning to class. Again, I discovered the instability of
my self-reliance and the discovery came in an unexpected way.

I taught two classes that day, navigating the dynamic
exchanges cautiously, and then claimed an air of nonchalant
confidence in my visit to the school office. I had every intention of informing my boss that I could manage teaching again.
Not yet healed, but well enough to do my job, I thought, and
I certainly didn't plan on telling him the extent to which my
mind had eroded. It was a good, old-fashioned, pull-yourself-
up-by-the-bootstraps moment. What actually happened came
as a complete surprise to both of us.

I sat down. He looked me straight in the eyes and
asked, "How are you?" Suddenly, I broke down like a child
again; racking sobs shook my whole body. He took my hands,
waited for a few minutes, and then asked the million dollar
question, "Why are you crying?"

And I knew why. I knew that something terrified me at
a molecular level. Failure, any sign that I lacked self-sufficiency
horrified me. All signs, however, pointed to a growing fissure in
the substratum of my preconceptions. What really terrified me

was that divine hands, against which I was simply powerless, had created that fissure into which I felt myself sliding.

***

I remember seeing Pablo Picasso's painting, "The Blind Man's Meal." It depicts a lanky and gaunt man sitting at a table. A bright blue scarf encircles his neck and a moody beret covers his young head. An empty dish and a pitcher rest on the wooden table. A cloth seems to be slipping off the table and into the man's lap, but his elbow keeps it pinned to the table. In his left hand, he holds a small loaf of bread with several bites taken out of it. His head inclines toward the pitcher, and the muscles of his neck stretch as though participating in the herculean task of grasping it in his right hand.

The composition of the piece, with its varied blues and the stiff figure at its center, arrests the imagination. The eyes–vacuous, hollow, and dark sockets–hopelessly press toward their object. Even the loaf depicts futility since the teeth bites are on the far side of the bread, as though someone besides this blind mendicant has been nibbling at the loaf without his knowing it.

I find this painting a powerful expression of our human condition, certainly mine. I was born dependent, born needy and frail and half-blind. Blind, even to my blindness, I aped

God. I would be sovereign. I would be the conqueror. I would be the redeemer of my own regret.

Thus, the water of life remained out of reach to me just as it did for Picasso's "Blind Man", and though I spent every waking moment straining toward it, satisfaction eluded me. Although I marshaled my troops and utilized every tool at my disposal in one enormous effort to reach the top of the mountain of self-sufficiency, I found no life-water there. Neither productivity nor pleasure, even healthy pleasure, could quench the dryness of my soul.

All the while, God called me into the wilderness where he had prepared a spring brimming with water cool enough to quench any man's thirst for a substantive life. I should have known better; instead of fleeing frailty, I should have recognized that I had inherited frailty.

***

When my boss suggested that I take an indeterminate time off from work, I felt a blanket of shame smother me. I tried to argue. I tried to beg. With deep, fatherly compassion he said, "Ben, I don't think you're listening to God."

"What?" I thought indignantly. I took pride in listening to God, but I felt my soul lurch and shiver like a boat striking suddenly against some mass in the darkness.

"I think you need to stay at home for however long it takes. You don't need to worry about your job, but you do need to stop fighting. You need to sit down and listen."

The truth? I feared stopping. I feared what I would hear in the inevitable stillness. Faced, alarmingly, with the realization that I lived in a house of cards, its collapse terrified me. The inescapable voice of God wormed through my mind, "The LORD said to him, 'Who gave human beings their mouths? Who makes them deaf or mute? Who gives them sight or makes them blind? Is it not I, the LORD?'"[3] What if the God I loved, the God whom I knew was a good God, full of grace and compassion[4] initiated my collapse?

If so, what to do? How to embrace calamity?

---

3   Exodus 4:11 NIV

4   Psalm 116:5

A Small Cup of Light

*"Où vous ai-je perdue,
mon imagerie piétinée?"*

Andre de Richaud
from "Le droit d'asile"

* "Where did I lose you,
my trampled fantasies?"

CHAPTER 3

Calamity Come

I was seven years old or so. Falling asleep in the thick, tropical air had proved difficult. I had stared at the ceiling and listened to my little brother breathing in the bunk beneath. His quiet breaths soothed my mind and I rode their rhythm over the edge of wakefulness into the land of dreams. While I dreamt, a dog crept beneath my outside window. In the quiet, thick night, he gathered up his lungs and barked as loudly as he could.

The bark woke me with such a start that I remember only feeling two sensations: hopelessness and terror colliding like two thunderclaps in my little brain. Suddenly paralyzed, even my breath froze and my eyes dilated. I don't remember being comforted, though I am sure my parents tried. I wanted to run. I wanted to hide. But the bark lodged inside my disoriented brain. I cried out in terror before melting into tears, sobbing. For many days thereafter, the bark of the dog outside my window darkened my world.

I am older now. I am wiser and more rational. But even now my shoulders lock up as I recall this episode in my life. Why? Because I am still afraid. The bark still reverberates in my mind and I know that it was a foreshadow of more shocking ones and darker paralyzations.

My sudden illness was a bark in the brain, but I faced many others before that. They take the form of miniature snapshots stuffed into the remote pockets of my memory along with the Arizona bunk beds, tile floor, and tire swing:

A miniature coffin painted black and lined starkly with white celtic crosses, waiting on the kitchen floor for a stillborn child whose premature passing left lasting grief, is one. I don't remember the family very well, but I remember the coffin.

A demolished car sputtering and smoking on the side of the road is another. I had turned prematurely in front of oncoming traffic and saw glass spray across my sister's face as a 4x4 pickup smashed into her passenger door. I was sixteen.

Scattered amongst the memories somewhere is a third snapshot, Julie, radiant and animated, a mother figure who vanished from history's plot in another car accident, the startling news passed to me over the phone.

And as I finger through the photos in my memory, I

encounter another painful scene. In this one, my little three year old girl strains, unable to breathe. I see her gasp for air, mouth wide, back arched, struggling with all her tiny might without result. I see her on the hospital bed, smallish and lost, hooked up to innumerable tubes.

For the nearly three weeks after my mind caught fire, the dilemma that kept barking at the back door of my mind was this: A good God is fine when life is tropically blissful, but what when the hurricane comes? Where is the safe haven then? What are we to do when chaos bangs against the windows and when the roof of reliability is ripped off?

What to do with all this suffering?

C.S. Lewis called pain God's megaphone. John Piper has called pain God's pedagogy. "God, I am listening. Teach me. Speak into this bewilderment."

***

After my meltdown in the office, everyone important to me encouraged me to stay home. My wife, father, mother, boss, and friends seemed to conspire against my ambitions. Unknown to them, I had begun to experience something more than mental erosion. Something on the back of my skull had begun vibrating. I could feel it like a hand.

Soon my head began bobbing involuntarily and tremors gradually took over my torso. And then my arms and even my legs shook. The shaking came and went at its leisure, but it came often. Sometimes the tremors took an hour to arrive but I could feel them growing in my body like an earthquake. My hands curled in on themselves and my tongue thickened in my mouth. I would sit like that for hours at a time.

When the tremors peaked, I was utterly helpless, hardly able even to hit my mouth with an eating utensil. Shame, again, smothered me. At dinner, my children tried to comfort and encourage me. I avoided their eyes. I angrily refused help. And when the tremors disappeared for a day or two, I took that as a sign I should return to work.

A week after my boss told me to take time off, I tried to come back. I even tried to coach a varsity boys' basketball game while the tremors coursed through my body. Sitting on that bench as I had done countless times before, I was struck again by my insufficiency. All the plays I had taught my players were gone from my recollection. All the technical details of the game were wiped clean from my mind. I couldn't stand and when I yelled, my clumsy tongue got in the way of coherent speech. My assistant, an amazing man who had handled the team and my sudden departure with great class, led the team to victory that night. I had nothing to do with it.

This time my boss sent me home with words more

firm: "Stay home and rest."

"I don't want to rest. I can do this! I can!" I rallied.

"No, you can't. I'm asking you to stay home. I want you to take whatever time necessary."

My boss was right, but anger welled up inside me. Defeat crouched in the darkness, mocking my life's unspoken credo: "Failure is not an option."

"Be still. Listen to God," he said.

In the days that followed, I felt the weight of involuntary house arrest and coaxed the anger inside me. I felt every right to be angry. Lying on the couch, besieged by tremors, entire cities in my mind suffering from blackout, I screamed at God in my heart; indeed, "...sorrow was within me like a convulsion."[1]

I suppose suffering is life's Mariana Trench. All 36,201 feet of it gash the ocean floor of our experience. Who are we to navigate its dark depths with a flashlight?

***

I recall playing in the sandbox under an African dusk when I was eight or so. Dad called me to him. He crouched down and watched the trees. I snuggled beneath his chin and crouched, too. In front of us a hen pecked for seeds. Her

---

1   Augustine, *Confessions*

chicks, scattered nearby, aimlessly pecked at the ground. One ruffled his feathers and wiggled for the sheer delight of it. Mother hen kept pecking the ground for insects or seeds. They were chickens. They did what chickens do.

Dad pointed into a tall tree across the yard, behind the car garage. "Look," he said.

"I can't see anything," I whispered.

"Wait and watch," he said.

We crouched, very still. I began to think of the sand-box and the waning light.

He lifted my chin and I looked up into the tree. Nothing. Then something, a movement like a cloak among the branches. With a wide spread of dark wings, a hawk material-ized.

I sensed something ominous.

The hen also sensed something. She perked up, saw the hawk, and began scuffling with her wings outstretched. Pandemonium ensued. The hen screamed. Her babies–plump and soft-feathered–scrambled, tripped, ran one way and then turned around to run in the other direction.

The hawk descended with power and intentionality and precision. He opened his talons and they squeezed around two little chicks that kicked mutely. The mother hen screamed some things at her attacker that I am sure would make an eight year old blush, but I was too busy crying to hear her. I, too, wanted to strike the brute and restore the chicks to their mother. Dad held me tight against his chest. The hawk vanished into the tall trees. Still, I could not bear to watch the chickens' grief and so I closed my eyes.

As a good father, Dad made me look. I saw the mother hen, bigger than before, her wings pulled close to her body. Then I noticed little beaks popping out from underneath. They trembled. She tousled their feathers one at a time and in a minute they ventured out from beneath her shelter.

Dad leaned into my ears and whispered a portion of Psalm 61 to me: "You have been a shelter for me, a strong tower from the enemy. I will abide in your tabernacle forever; I will trust in the shelter of your wings."

Hawk and hen, God made them both. That troubled evening scene illustrated a rich Augustinian doctrine: "O Lord our God, under the shadow of thy wings let us hope–defend us and support us. Thou wilt bear us up when we are little and even down to our gray hairs wilt carry us. For our stability, when it is in thee, is stability indeed; but when it is in ourselves, then it is all unstable."[2]

---

2   Augustine, *Confessions*

***

My stability dissolved under the strain of suffering. In my suffering, I forgot that pain has a context. It is framed by the Master Storyteller. I am imagined: before I kicked against my mother's womb, before the nurse pricked my heel and I cried out, before I threw a snowball and squealed with delight, God imagined all of it.

He imagined the death of grubs and the death of the chicks that ate them. Such pain is part of his story. Thomas Merton suggested that the mystery of God eclipses our suffering. Pain is no case against God. No matter the cause. No matter the degree. Suffering does not call into question the existence of a good God; rather, it calls into question our lives. Who am I? Why am I here?

I am a part of his story. I am the epiphany of God. I am a character whose life events have a purpose for me and for the story. Every event has purpose in the author's larger design, even the bark of a dog, the death of a baby bird, or a small black coffin for a stillborn child. He knows the falling of a sparrow and he knew the collapse of a mind. God does not look at our suffering from afar. It is an intimate event to him. He is the author of every detail, speaking the suffering as it occurs.

John of the Cross knew suffering, and he knew who

spoke the suffering. His father died when he was seven years old and his older brother died two years later. He endured significant persecution in his life, including being arrested and even kidnapped. John's kidnappers held him in a small cell just large enough for his body where he had to stand on tiptoe to read his breviary by the light that passed through a little hole from an adjoining room. They whipped him publicly once a week. They fed him bread and scraps of fish, but the friars who guarded his cell passed him paper and he composed his most famous poem "Spiritual Canticle" and some other shorter poems.

John's suffering was significant. He knew what it was to be swallowed. He called it the dark night of the soul, a night like the one Jonah experienced when he was swallowed and left with no other choice but to listen.

Iain Matthew, in his book *The Impact of God*, suggests that what we call normal life is an anesthetic against the reality of our distance from God. In other words, our passing day-to-day routines act as cloud cover that shrouds our vision and keeps us from recognizing our absolute smallness and isolation. The sudden onslaught of suffering exposed John of the Cross's inner self to the raw ache for a God who was utterly out of reach; at least, out of reach by our own efforts.

Yes, we are raw. Yes, we are in the dark belly of a

whale. Yes, we ache. Who can be Jesus' "little sunbeam" at such a time? Would Jesus even want such a thing? He is after much more than happiness in our lives. He is after a sustaining joy and he will give us that joy by giving us himself, whether through the small gifts of life that bring us gladness or through the dark night of suffering. Sweeping affliction under the rug of our heart, therefore, is simple denial, an act of cowardice, and an act of ungratefulness. We must dare to look it square in the eyes.

Job, one of the most godly men to grace the pages of Scripture, spoke profoundly to our human state when he said, "For God has made my heart weak, and the Almighty terrifies me; because I was not cut off from the presence of darkness, and he did not hide deep darkness from my face."[3]

Pain is a deep darkness before my eyes. I don't know how to talk about it. I can't even write about it without approaching it with sidelong glances or describing it as through a prism, from differing angles. But I'm surrounded by it.

Suffering prompts a kind of spiritual vertigo and it becomes impossible to keep our feet firmly planted. Normalcy, or what we've come to call normal, suddenly seems out of reach. In my own suffering, I wanted to be through with it all, to be normal again.

---

3   Job 24:16-17

***

I approached only the one month anniversary since my mind caught fire, but I still longed to wake up from the nightmare, to put my feet on the ground and stand without thinking about every muscle's assignment. The tremors gradually increased their frequency and intensity. Ah, to lose my shuffling step, to repair my broken-backed confidence, to eat, work, sleep, and sit in traffic jams like normal people.

In some respects, a heightened awareness of normal existence progressing all around me, despite my sudden abnormalities, acted as an enormous sheet of glass suddenly separating me from the passing world. I stood caged on the sidewalk of life, unable to break the glass or reach through it.

Caged.

Others peered back at me through the glass, but my tremors and I were now strange to them, removed, abstract, difficult to understand. I pressed my hands against the barrier, but it would not move. I pressed my ear against it and heard the sounds of regular life that I so missed. When others laughed, their happiness seemed as removed from me as one watching a film. I felt studied, interesting and isolated. Frantic, I wanted normal again. But what was normal? Coursing tremors? No. A mind gone dark? Not that either.

I could not move my legs well. I could not move my hands. My body trembled and nobody knew why. While the world woke to its plodding labors, greasing the axels of ambition, I remained in my hermit's hut clutching my blanket of self-pity and remorse. All glimpses of youthful vigor, vibrancy, and easy carriage were a twisting needle in my soul. I did not want the sight of a busy world to amplify my miserable loneliness, my weakness, and my uncontrollable trembling, so I avoided windows. The stagnant waters of my mind began to stink.

A Small Cup of Light

"Thou mastering me
God!"

Gerard Manley Hopkins
from "The Wreck of the Deutschland"

CHAPTER 4

God, Loose And At Large

I returned to school one week after my boss told me to stay home, roughly three weeks after my son found me in the snow. With weak legs and an even weaker mind, I lurched back to teaching, working harder than ever to appear calm and collected and competent. I don't know if my stubborn pride drove me back or my deep-seated longing for business as usual pulled me there. Perhaps both forces worked, one pulling the rope around my neck and the other lashing me from behind. In either case, I pretended everything was back to normal, that I was normal, that I was myself again.

Nature's storehouse of lessons should have served as an adequate caution against this illusion of calm. Growing up on a small river, I knew by experience that the slow surfaces, curling and twisting over dark deeps, were most to be feared. The rapids at least showed where the rocks waited. Though one might be dashed against a rock, at least he saw it coming and he knew what to avoid. But the deceptive calm tempted little boys to take swims and the deceptive deeps hid undercurrents vigorous enough to pin a strong man down against the river's gravel bed.

When I was in high school and enjoying the vaulting strength of youth, my family took some river rookies on a canoe ride. To no one's surprise, the rookies drifted into the curve of a river's bend and a waiting willow's branches. Their canoe capsized and we helped them to shore, only to discover that one man had lost his wallet. Accustomed to the river, I dove back in and scouted the scene for the object. There it sat, lodged under a log ten feet down, friendless like a stranger in a foreign land. I came up to catch a breath and dove down again. I had caught the wallet in my hand when an undercurrent grabbed me, twisted me around the waist and thrust me beneath the log.

I had faced undercurrents before, but nothing this strong, nothing this inevitable. I struggled against the current as anyone would, but every struggle jammed me more firmly under the pressing weight of that log. With my arms jammed to my side and my head crushed between the river rock and the log, I held my breath and felt my lungs burn. I kicked. Nothing. I wondered what my family was thinking and hoped someone would jump in to save me. And then I hoped they wouldn't jump so there wouldn't be two of us stuck and fumbling for life at the bottom. I wondered if they realized how long I had been under.

My breath was almost gone when a thought struck me. What if I gave in to the pull? What if I let the undertow have its way. Might it sweep me out from under the log? So I swiveled beneath the log, moving with the undercurrent. I did not know if it would work, but being desperate, I had no other option. Within moments and with almost no effort on my part, the undercurrent pulled me through to the other side, and with one swift push off the riverbed, I rose to light and to air and to family and–finally, with a gasp–to life.

***

Despair is an undertow more terrifying, more pressing than a river's undertow, powerful though it may be. It's like a blind force pushing not just the body, but the soul against the river's gravelly bed. I feared despair and the corresponding realization of my dependency and so I kept fighting. If I had embraced my dependency earlier, my story might be different.

Though I tried to teach, tried to resume my old routines, I staggered through my days in search of air and light for my soul, in search of hope. All my aspirations narrowed to one pinpoint: to regain my former self. I begged God to give me myself again.

The thought did not cross my mind, at the time, that I was being selved in the womb of suffering. I was becoming a new self. I was being birthed, somehow, again, in the darkness, feeling the constrictive pressures of labor. The anguish squeezed my spiritual lungs and I floundered in despair.

When I was at home, my wife and children tried, mostly unsuccessfully, to live a hushed life in the margins of our house. They giggled and fought and sang, barreling headlong into life while only momentarily tiptoeing past their father. Our house is small and the sounds of their lives surged up through the floorboards or flapped like birds through the vents in the walls. I tried. I tried to welcome them into my strange world. Sometimes they even cautiously approached to peek into the grove of loneliness where a man in the likeness of their father puttered around and where storm-clouds gathered unannounced. The tremors, the anxiety, the fatigue, the anger, the bewilderment all were new and uninvited, ushering me into loneliness in the midst of their radiant life.

Four weeks into my health crisis, I resigned from coaching. No one asked me to resign. I knew I had to. I couldn't coach them to the championship with a mind bereft of all its basketball knowledge. Honestly, I thought about resigning from teaching too. All my technical knowledge, not just basketball knowledge, was wiped clean. I had no recollection of dates or historical names. Even the names of my students and colleagues were slipping off the table of my mind and my grammatical knowledge was gone completely.

"One thing at a time," I thought. So I gathered the team, my assistant coach, and the athletic director in my classroom to give a short speech. The long and the short of it was this: "I'm done. God's still in charge. You're in good hands. I love you, but I'm resigning."

On the night of the semi-finals, I was so angry that I asked my wife if we could go somewhere busy and loud to distract me. We found a restaurant that fit the bill and ate in relative silence. The restuarant chaos rattled me, crashing violently into the walls of my mind, and exacerbated the tremors, but it worked. I was distracted, at least a bit.

Toward the end of the meal, my phone rang. An update. I could hear the pandemonium in the background and my heart started racing. My longing to be on the sideline, marshaling the troops, outmaneuvering the opponent, rose up like a goiter in my throat. I heard the final thirty seconds, including the game winning shot by our opponent. My team lost. Without me. My absence was another failure.

I hung up the phone.

"We lost...could you hear the crowd in the background? It was so crazy loud," I said to my wife, trying to smile.

She smiled and took my hand. She helped me navigate on my still unsteady legs through the tables toward the door. She drove me home in sad darkness. In my memory, the drive seems quiet and lonely, but the tremors in my hands and head and legs stayed close to me in the gloom.

I sensed an isolation as I crawled under the covers later. Distance from my team. Distance from my students. Space growing between me and those I loved and didn't love: they shared similarly curious looks, they shared similarly unhelpful phrases to dodge the topic. We all sidestepped. Evasive maneuvers, twirling like ungainly ballerinas around the anomaly none of us could understand, none of us could name. I was being quietly islanded by this nameless affliction.

I lay under the covers when we arrived home and I prayed in the silent darkness, a rambling cry for help formed by a racing mind. Trying to pray with any clarity was like strapping a bird to a cat's back and demanding the cat walk in a straight line, but I made the classic bargain with God anyways: "If you heal me, then I'll work even harder for you. Just heal me and get me back to normal so I can go about your business again." I prayed, knowing that God listens to our infantile fumblings. He even answers.

***

A few days later, however, I was home again. The tremors debilitated my ability to think straight and my empty mental vaults made it just too difficult to teach. My boss and I met with a dear friend who would serve as a long term substitute. She was incredibly competent, but during that meeting my anger at this new development roiled beneath my calm exterior.

I sat on the couch afterward and groaned in my anguish. I prayed angrily for healing. I demanded my old self back. Though I thought I wanted to be healed so I could serve God, my true master was Productivity, a master whose malice knows no limits when he is not satiated. It didn't register with me that maybe what I was doing in God's name wasn't as essential as what God was doing in his name. God was about his business on me; nevertheless, spending day after day without putting my hand to the plow at work meant more whips on my soul's back. I could feel the flesh peeling and starting to fester. Productivity had become my Golem, but I did not know it.

According to legend, a Golem was a being created out of dust to help in time of need. Only the most holy of rabbis, those close enough to God to gain access to the secret wisdom of creation, were capable of creating such a being. Jewish tradition tells the story of a 16th century rabbi, Juda Loew ben Bezel, who created a Golem to defend the Prague ghetto from attack. Unfortunately, an unavoidable complication arose. Since the Golem was not intelligent, like all Golems, it performed the requested task literally but over time it became uncooperative. When it threatened the destruction of its maker and many others besides, Juda ben Bezel barely succeeded to immobilize it.

Juda ben Bezel was not the only one to create such a being. Gaon R. Eliyahu Ba'al Shem apparently forged one, too, by making a creature of clay, inscribing the word *emet*–truth– on its forhead. When he said the name of God, the Golem came to life. But the Golem grew too large and the Gaon feared it might destroy the world, so he commanded it to bend down and he removed the first letter from its forhead. *Emet*– truth–became *met*–death–and the Golem toppled over. In an ironic twist, however, the Golem came crashing down on top of Gaon R. Eliyahu Ba'al Shem, the very man who created him.

It seems to me that some Golems, which we ourselves conjure, usually end up destroying us. Most of them are formed to save us from relational or professional failure, but the nastiest Golems are those built to save us from spiritual failure. Those are the Golems that mimic God. They act just similarly enough to how God acts to be able to deceive us into feeling like we are actually serving him. But as a man once said, "Close is still a miss." I had no idea I had created my own Golem. It took a mentor to show me.

I visited him one day to seek his advice about my affliction and he asked me a rather strange question: "What is your definition of an idol?"

I gazed at his grizzled beard and bushy eyebrows. "Anything that I love more than I love God," I replied, as though in Sunday School again.

He seemed disappointed, calling my answer both uncreative and inaccurate. "Everyone says that, but it's only partially true. An idol is actually anything that promises to deliver us from death." He paused as the fragments of my mind began to coalesce. "What is death to you, Ben?"

I knew exactly what death was to me.

"Failure is death. Any form of failure, even disappointing someone, is death to me," I said.

"And what promises to save you from that death?"

A myriad of things came to mind, my hyper-productivity, my perfectionism, my strict organization that verged on OCD. They formed the arms, torso, and head of my own personal Golem built to save me from destruction. It rose up before me, looming large, and I saw behind it a destructive trail littered behind it.

"Dear God," I said. And then, "Let's cut the idol down."

"You want to cut down an idol built of productivity by doing something, by being productive?" he laughed. "What do you think life is about, man?"

I was stunned but he kept talking, speaking into my bewilderment with gentleness this time, "You aren't what you do, Ben. Your identity is found in Christ. You don't have to prove anything to God. You can't. There's great peace in that, a peace that seems to have evaded you for some time. God just wants you. Sit with him. Be still. Everything you do should spring naturally from the joy you've found by being with God."

I thought I knew what life was about. Like Martha in Luke 10, I leaned into distraction more than I leaned into Christ. All the while, I sincerely thought that my worship of business was a virtue. Christ would have said to me what he said to Martha, "Martha, Martha, you are worried and troubled about many things. But one thing is needed, and Mary has chosen that good part, which will not be taken away from her." Unaware that the God I was serving with productivity did not exact the toll for his grace that I was paying so dearly, I blundered into two essential questions: what does God want from me and who am I when life goes sideways?

And then I knew that my Golem would not go quietly

nor easily. I knew that I would have to revert to trickery and that I might be harmed in the process. My Golem, a companion since my youth, was now a nanny who sang over me the lullabies of self-reliance. I had not seen that this Golem caused me to sweat through each night. How ironic that the thing I had created to defend me from harm had grown dangerously close to destroying my universe. I just hadn't known it.

Soon after this encounter with my mentor, I wrote a letter to a friend whose impact on my life has been immeasurable. His wife died in an accident, relatively early in their marriage, and his quiet strength inspired many of us. In the letter, I summarized my case and asked his advice. This, in part, was his response:

Dear Ben,

Looking back at my life I recognize God's gracious hand upon me and yet there are many times of darkness/silence and what feels to me like failure. I knew that you had been struggling, but not the depths as you describe them. I have no special insight to share, but I believe that your path is one that God sometimes sets our feet upon. I pray that you will be able to catch glimpses of him in the darkness, that you will be upheld by a deep trust that he is with you and that it is good to be where you are until he moves you along. Please keep me informed as to your journey.

Scrawled at the bottom of the page was the verse, Jonah 2:8. I looked it up and thought perhaps he made a mistake. Verse nine says, "When my life was ebbing away, I remembered you, Lord, and my prayer rose to you, to your holy temple." Surely, that was what he meant to write. Or Jonah 2:7 would have been appropriate, "To the roots of the mountains I sank down; the earth beneath barred me in forever. But you, Lord my God, brought my life up from the pit." Instead, he wrote Jonah 2:8: "Those who regard worthless idols forsake their own mercy."

I had never mentioned idols to him.

***

It seemed my Golem was being exposed from multiple angles. I slowly recognized that my Golem had protected me from showing signs of weakness and insulated me from long draughts at the well of grief. I had no idea, however, what my Golem was really keeping me from: a naked encounter with God.

All those tactics to hide my vulnerability and expunge weakness were feeble attempts to delay the one encounter my soul longed for the most and my heart feared the most.

I would have denied it at the time, of course, but it takes no great sleuth to deduce that my willingness to encounter God remained limited to relatively painless life experiences. If a person truly desires God, he must welcome whatever means God uses to initiate that encounter, whether laughter or grief.

My protests against tremors, mental erasure, and fatigue exposed my predisposition to meet God on my terms. But God is "loose and at large"[1] and God has proved himself an overwhelming God, unthwarted and determined, bent on doing whatever he must do to bring people to himself.

He was not simply out to expose my idols, he was calling me up and out into a mystery, to a place I could not see, where I would be emptied. He was pressing in on me until I sat still and listened to his quiet voice in my own personal wilderness. He warned as much in Isaiah 45:6-7 when he said, "I am The Lord, and there is no other; I form the light and create darkness, I make peace and create calamity; I, The Lord, do all these things."

The mental erasure, the tremors, the frailty constituted my own little darkness. I stumbled in it, terrified of the truth: "I, The Lord, do all these things."

---

1   J.I. Packer, *Knowing God*

*"All I know is
a door into the dark."*

Seamus Heaney
from "The Forge"

CHAPTER 5
A Door Into The Dark

Then, rocking tremors set in. They would begin at my feet and course through my legs, up my trunk and into my neck and arms. My hands would curl inward even more severely than before and I would stoop with my head cocked to one side, rocking my whole body. Even sitting was a violent activity.

Normalcy became a disorienting and aggravating ringing in my ears. Surrounded by happy, galloping children, I found a hidden passage into a dark corner of my heart where the ringing quieted. I uncovered a small trap door there, unlatched it and crawled through. What I found on the other side was small and hard but living—tissue growing like a tumor. While the children recounted their school days and conversation leapt around me, I sat at the table, fumbled with utensils, gingerly lifted food into my mouth, and brooded.

Like a good surgeon, I kept probing my soul's tumor with a scalpel, making small incisions here and there to see what kind of fluid leaked out of it. The tumor hardened by the day as I lost motor and mental function. Tremors came and went at their leisure, sucking my body's strength dry most of the time.

I tried to live my life: waking and dressing each morning, pretending to participate in family life, acting engaged at birthday parties. To prevent any awkwardness, I focused all my strength on restraining the tremors for ten to twenty-minutes at a time while I visited with others. I, and the legion of my infirmities, was an intrusion on normal life. Tremors were an unwanted limitation to normal pursuits and others simply didn't know what to do or say.

Once, my dear mother visited, as she did often, this time bringing lunch and a book of artwork. With the kids gone at school and my wife at work, I sat at the table while Mom shared beautiful paintings with me. She tenderly turned page after page while I tried to feed myself.

"They're beautiful, aren't they?"

"Yes," I said.

I struggled to embrace transcendent radiance in those paintings, but my inadequacy and fear festered like boils on my heart, boils that needed lancing.

She prayed for me before leaving–prayed for peace and rest–but long after she left, I avoided confronting my frailty and fears. I forged ahead day after day, trying to conquer illness with self-reliance and good old fashioned willpower. I even attended larger events, sometimes by myself if the tremors were absent more than a week.

One night, I attended a banquet. Tremors surfaced during it—wave upon wave. I tried with relative success to contain them throughout. Afterward, I hastily excused myself, feeling the strength sapping rapidly from my legs. I shuffled through the dark, skirting human contact to mitigate my personal shame, and stumbled to the car, but I couldn't pick up the keys. My fingers wouldn't work. I fumbled with my cell phone and finally pushed one number: speed-dial home. When my wife answered, I tried to speak, but the shaking of my head scrambled the words on my tongue. They only came in lurches.

"Trouble," I said after some effort. "I'm in." Those two words took even more time to vocalize.

My wife called my parents for help because they were close by. When my mom and dad drove up, they found me sitting, helpless, in the driver's seat of our van in an empty parking lot. They assisted me into the passenger's side, and Dad drove me home while Mom followed with their car. I can only imagine what was passing through her mind, what fears she fought with prayer as we drove.

Slumped in the seat next to Dad, with my head lilting

to the side and my mouth parted uncontrollably, I reverted to my childhood self. I thought like a child. I spoke like a child. I felt an overwhelming urge to lie down with my head in Mom's or Dad's lap like I used to when I was young. Dad helped me into my bed when we arrived home and then drove away with Mom, only to lie awake in their own bed, stare into the night, and pray.

I felt George MacDonald's agonized cry echo poignantly in my soul: "My harvest withers. Health, my means to live—all things seem rushing straight into the dark. But the dark is still God."[1]

I lay in bed as an invalid that night, not knowing if my miserable state was permanent, not knowing if it would subside in due time. I lay alone in a wilderness of darkness, hardly able to see my own hand before my face, searching desperately for a small light by which I could find my way. I felt I was being unmade.

***

Since I was old enough to speak, I have been taught that Jacob was the third of three key patriarchs. Jacob—like me, a get-er-done kind of man—did whatever it took to achieve his

---

1 George MacDonald, *A Book of Strife in the Form of The Diary of an Old Soul*

ambition, even conning his father and duping his brother. He received the inheritance he wanted, but had to live on the run for some time.

When Jacob camped alone one night under the stars, he did not know that his life would soon be unmade. In the early morning hours, a man crossed the stream and approached him. They locked forearms and Jacob knew the overwhelming determination of an unthwarted God. They wrestled, hand to hand, sweat against sweat, for many hours. Jacob held his own. Although he was wrestling the Angel of The Lord, Jacob would not relent. They grappled through the night. Finally, the Angel had had enough...and simply touched Jacob.

Hours of struggle finished in an instant. "Just as he crossed over Penuel the sun rose on him, and he limped on his hip," the Scripture says. Jacob had felt the finger of God and would walk with a limp for the rest of his life.

That touch transformed him into an infirm man. In Latin, infirm means "not strong," a word denoting all things undesirable to me. Jacob, like many, wanted nothing to do with weakness, but Jacob's world became an infirmary from that point on. Jacob's customary framework for life, his gaudy self-reliance and ambition, scattered like pheasants flushed. As Li-Young Lee so poignantly asked, "Who lay down at evening and woke at night a stranger to himself?[2]" Jacob did.

I did.

***

Like Jacob, something inside me still refused to raise the white flag of truce even seven weeks after my son found me burrowing into the snow. Though I had difficulty forming words, let alone thinking or reading them again, I fought to maintain a simple vocabulary in my head. I hung on every word spoken to me and let it marinate in my mind. I longed for people to speak slowly and carefully, not flippantly as people so often do.

I paced the living room of my mind reciting the names of people I loved, picturing their faces. Even my friends and students were sometimes nameless, like grocery clerks. When I remembered to, I carried the church directory with me and read names on the drive to worship services. I was harried by the pressing terror of forgetting, and frightened by the growing webs in the back rooms of my mind.

I spent most of my hours on the couch. I remember the fabric of the couch pressed into my leg and the way the sunlight passed along the couch's back while I lay there, log heavy and sagged in my soul. Laughter still filtered through

---

2   Li-Young Lee, "From Another Room"

closed doors, but worry gnawed like a rat at the frayed edges of my mind.

The end of February approached and I was still not back to work. Fatigue begat lethargy. And lying prone on the couch day after day, I felt a thousand gallons of bile swelling up into my throat. So I slid one leg over the edge of the couch and let it hit the ground. I slid the other one along the cushion and it followed the first heavily like a stump. With two feet flat on the floor, I pulled the rest of my limp body to follow.

I eyed the door which shut out the winter and considered what enormous effort it would take to actually fight atrophy by standing and walking. But something goaded me toward the door. The desire to reclaim the old powers of physical and mental control urged me onward. I wanted business as usual again and any suggestion that a new normalcy, a different normal, was beginning to form repulsed me. Frailty was an unwanted guest and I would refuse him permanent residence.

Sliding one foot after another, I inched toward the door, pausing once my hand grasped the knob. How cold was the air? How far could I possibly walk? And how would I navigate the stairs? Determined, I stepped into the cold and carefully navigated down the stairs holding the rail in one hand. Finally, I stood flat-footed and exhausted on the sidewalk.

I eyed the mailbox which leaned into the street some

fifty feet away. I took a step, sliding my toes along the concrete and then my reluctant heel. Then I slid the toes of my other foot and that heel followed. Imagine the fool I must have looked, inching down the walk, bunched over and doddering like an old man. When I reached the mailbox, I rested my weary hands upon its sloping back and leaned with it into the road, wondering how I would ever make it back to the house.

Every day, I braved the cold air, the looming stairs, and the fifty feet of walkway. When I pulled myself back into the house and collapsed onto the microfiber of my familiar couch, the fatigue seeped from my muscles into my bloodstream where it flooded the chambers of my heart.

I could feel depression's hooks sunk into my heart, dragging it toward the edge of some unnamed abyss.

***

Lying on the couch, increasingly alarmed at my mental and physical fatigue, the myriad thoughts and fears clambered like bats in the attic of my mind. They banged against its thin housing like the cloud of bats that sometimes poured out from beneath the eaves of our house in Kenya and pulsated into the night sky. I did not sleep well. The rapid nature of my collapse offered something very real to fear. Feeling marooned and helpless only amplified the fear.

I confided this feeling in a friend one day and he told me to read Isaiah, chapter 50. To my great chagrin, the chapter offered no comfort in my distress.

"Who among you fears The Lord?
Who obeys the voice of his servant?
Who walks in darkness and has no light?
Let him trust in the name of The Lord
And rely upon his God.
Look, all you who kindle a fire,
Who encircle yourselves with sparks:
Walk in the light of your fire and in
the sparks you have kindled—
This you shall have from my hand:
You shall lie down in torment."[3]

Isaiah, the prophet, wrote that God takes us into desert places without light, and he will not allow us to bring light into the desert nor will he allow us to strike stones together to start a spark. God promises torment to those who plant torches in the sand to encircle themselves and keep the beasts at bay. "Face the darkness with nothing but me," says the Lord. Simply sit.

There is, apparently, a greater torment than sitting in

---

3   Isaiah 50:10-11

the dark, feeling exceptionally alone, and listening to the bats flap and squeak. If we ignore the bats or try to comfort ourselves with the brightness of myriad distractions, then torment will be our bedding. If we try to comfort ourselves in our need instead of leaning fully on our God and Savior, God promises to make us taste that need full force.

I read Isaiah 50 and recognized myself. I was the man lighting fires to comfort himself in the desert darkness. I was the man chasing every promise of relief. Still, I could not bring myself to sit still and listen.

"Ah, God, deliver me from this wilderness!" I cried inside. "What good is a lame life?" And so I squirmed in my soul.

***

Then a new twist to my health crisis emerged nearly two months into my collapse: I started falling asleep at unexpected times. Sometimes at dinner I felt sleep pull over my mind like a sheet and my head would hit the table within seconds. After some time I could recognize the signs of oncoming sleep. When I finally saw them, I realized that I had less than a fifteen-second window between the recognition of its signs and actual sleep.

When I felt sleep coming, I would stand to walk to the couch, but fatigue made me slow. Sometimes I didn't make it to the couch before sleep arrived; I would buckle to the floor, my knees crumpled under me, my arms limp, and my forehead planted on the carpet. I tried night after night to reach the couch, but repeatedly failed. The first few times alarmed my wife and children, but then the sleep slumps became a source of laughter.

Humor became a kind of relief valve in our home, momentarily warding off mounting fears. Tenderness coupled with laughter became a balm even to me. When my family called me "tripod" and imitated my collapses, I usually found it funny. But one evening, my sleep problems became a gateway to familial conflict, a trap door through which my anger sprang.

I sat in the living room trying to read while my daughter worked on her homework next to me. She stumbled through her assignment, asking for help repeatedly. I did not have the mental fortitude to keep up with her assignment and told her so, but she kept asking. Finally, she asked for help again and, with gritted teeth, I told her to do her own work. I closed my eyes in frustration and the next thing I knew, my wife was yelling my name and slapping my leg. It all seemed so uncalled for. When I opened my eyes in anger, I saw my daughter looking at me imploringly as though she needed help again.

"Do your own work!" I yelled.

Tears burst from her eyes. "Oh, Daddy!" she cried.

My wife knelt down and took my hands in her own. With remarkable calm, she whispered, "Honey, you've been asleep for forty-five minutes." My wife, though stable and characteristically a problem-solver, began to betray her growing fear through her eyes. Was this permanent? Would she be saddled with four children and an invalid husband?

Her words stunned me. It could not be. I felt embarrassed. What had been a nuisance, these unpredictable sleep attacks, was now worthy of alarm. I underwent a twenty-four hour sleep study where they taped electrodes to what seemed like every square inch of my head. I slept through the night and they recorded the activity of my mind. I spent the following day taking regular naps.

They found that while one part of my mind drifted predictably into REM sleep, another part of my mind climbed into hyper-active mode as if to make up for the "slacker" portion. For that reason, I could not tell, sometimes, whether I was asleep or awake. They called it Idiopathic Narcolepsy and assured me that there wasn't much I could do. Over the next few weeks, they would try various medications to keep me awake during the day so that I would sleep better at night, but with little effect.

What a strange feeling of helplessness to be already

two months with this "illness", to be so close to answers, to have so much information, and yet find no solutions. This Idiopathic Narcolepsy compounded my mental and physical fatigue and accelerated my decline into a second infancy.

I required help to walk, sometimes even to pick up food with my fork, and the tremors only increased. I felt myself slipping beyond the reaches of panic, or alarm, and settling into a kind of spiritual lethargy that turned the world slow, brown, and meaningless.

***

One day, a friend showed up at the door. He was a father-figure in my life.

"I'm taking you on a road trip," he said. "We're going up to the St. Joe River."

He helped me off the couch and half-carried me down the stairs and into his truck. I felt his hands against my ribs and waves of self-loathing crashed upon my mental shores. I was infantile, pathetic, burdensome, needy, and, yes, weak.

Weak. I hated that word.

I hunched in the passenger seat. I thought I'd give him a warning at the outset: "It's hard to talk," I said.

"That's alright," he replied. "Quiet is good."

So that's what we had. Quiet.

The color and light sped by, darting between trees, glancing off the snow while the clear, bright, vast sky cupped over the world like an enormous blue egg. I sat inside the egg, trying to focus, wanting nothing more than strength to fly and flee. The truck carried its cabin full of silence along back roads, through small country towns, Valleyford and Rockford, before my friend finally spoke.

"How are you feeling?"

My brain scurried along the floor of responses like a mouse desperately searching for some bit of cheese, some token to offer to this unwanted question. I felt a shallow surge of revulsion.

But at any rate, I was honest. "I feel like a child." I paused to regroup and gather all my strength to say more. "I feel small."

I stared out the window, avoiding eye contact.

"What a beautiful place to be," he whispered.

Stunned, I turned to cast a condemning eye upon him. He smiled. A broad grin had spread across his face and I was dumbstruck. "Perhaps he has lost his mind," I thought, convinced that he did not understand the impoverishment that came with this lonely smallness. Worse yet, he had no idea what it felt like to be castrated, unmanned, in this fashion.

He spoke again and quoted Scripture: "Lord, my heart

is not haughty, nor my eyes lofty. Neither do I concern myself with great matters, nor with things too profound for me. Surely I have calmed and quieted my soul, like a weaned child with his mother; like a weaned child is my soul within me."[4]

I looked out the window and considered the psalmist. His words were a balm, but I could not reconcile such words with my current helplessness. Little did I understand.

Little.

Ignorant.

I did not know at the time that Psalm 131 was a Song of Ascent, also called a Song of Degrees or Song of Steps, a pilgrim song for those climbing toward Jerusalem to celebrate a high feast. It is a pilgrim's song.

"Like a weaned child is my soul within me."

I, too, was on pilgrimage. I, too, was climbing toward Jerusalem to celebrate. I, too, was learning to accept from God, like a weaned child, whatever he so desired to give me.

But I didn't know it at the time. In that moment, I only felt incongruities in my heart and mind. Like a note sung clear and long, but out of tune, this Psalm of comfort made me squirm.

We reached Saint Maries, Idaho, and turned to follow the St. Joe River along the foothills, then gradually wound up

---

4   Psalm 131

and up into the mountains toward the tiny town of Avery—a climb I will not soon forget.

The road followed the meandering river and clung to the edge of cliffs at times, while at others it would lose sight of the river altogether before meeting the waters again around a bend in the road. Sometimes the water crept beneath sheets of snow-covered ice that reached their fingers across the water's surface. Sometimes the water churned over and around large boulders and through the narrows, voraciously whorling into wildness.

Though we drove up into the mountains and deeper into the cold expanse of snow, I felt something unthawing in me. I felt a crack in the ice of my heart. A very small, hairline crack, but a crack nonetheless. Who was to say whether this crack signaled the onset of spring in my spirit or the first, near-silent popping under my feet before the ice would give way and I would sink into the dark abyss, forever lost, forever cold.

Heavy snowfall blocked the roads past Avery so we turned around. At one particular bend in the river, I asked my friend to stop. He found a pull-off, and we stood at the edge of the road, gazing over the barrier at the river winding away. I took out my camera and pulled my friend next to me. I tremulously lifted the camera out in front of us, with the river churning behind and the sun beaming above, and snapped a picture.

The return drive took longer, as I recall. We lingered and, at one point, just beyond Huckleberry Mountain, we saw a moose out in the fields. We pulled over to watch it for a moment. Mired up nearly to its belly in the thick snow with no idea we were watching, it churned and plunged through the thick whiteness: a desperate, awkward, gangly effort.

I felt pity rise in my throat and recognized the animal's feeble attempts. The deep snow stretched wide under open expanse. The moose wanted the shelter of the woods, but it had much too far to go, so it stopped and sweated and shivered under the strain. Then it lunged again, but tripped, stumbling into the snow.

As we watched, I thought of the deep coldness that surrounded me. It penetrated my bones. I thought of the fatigue that came from trying to live and the fear that came from not trying. I thought of the cold grip that slid up my legs towards my heart. Something in me cried out for the moose. I wanted so badly to aid it in its lunge for freedom, yet I could do nothing but watch the solitary battle: a dark, heavy form on a field of white.

We climbed back into the truck and drove home in silence, leaving the moose to its lonely struggle. When we arrived home, my friend helped me back into the house and onto the couch. My children greeted us radiantly and my wife kissed me on the cheek.

"How was it?" she asked after he left.

I remembered the bright sun dancing on the snow, the light leaping among the trees, and the whirling water. I remembered the agonizing moose staggering alone in the deep snow. I remembered Psalm 131: "Surely I have calmed and quieted my soul, like a weaned child with his mother; like a weaned child is my soul within me." As I recalled the day's journey, a match was struck somewhere inside me, and a spurt of light sprang up in the darkened corner of my heart.

"It was beautiful," I whispered. And somehow I meant it.

A Small Cup of Light

"Dear God, be good to me;
Thy sea is so wide,
And my boat is so small."

A Breton Fisherman's Prayer

CHAPTER 6

A Red Chair In Falling Snow

One Sunday in March, the tremors pulsing violently on my
brain made my hands go limp. My head listed like a ship
without ballast. It nodded with my whole body. Sitting in the
church pew was especially difficult that day and so I wandered
downstairs, making my way slowly along the rail. The church
service was muffled above me as I shuffled to a seat in a corner
and rested. When I knew the sermon was winding down, I
rose and began the long climb up to the sanctuary. My halting
steps, one after another, slowed with each stair. At the top of
the flight, and in plain sight of many people, my foot caught
and I lurched to the floor. I pushed myself off the ground
before anyone could come to my aid and put on a good face for
those who looked concerned.

It worked. They turned to hear the sermon's close while
I trembled in my shame. Shame. Brokeness. Insufficiency again.
I worked my way to the rest of the family and heard nothing

for the rest of the sermon except the persistent whispering of my shame. I ate and drank the sacraments, but the whispering continued.

At the end of our service, the congregation stood with hands raised to sing the *Gloria Patri*. I stood too, albeit with difficulty. I raised my hands with the rest. And I sang with them: "Glory be to the Father, and to the Son, and to the Holy Ghost. As it was in the beginning, is now, and ever shall be, for ever and ever. Amen. Amen."

As I stood there with them and sang the words, I realized quite vividly that three-hundred empty hands surrounded me. My hands were empty too. All our hands raised to God in a profoundly worshipful gesture, as if everyone under that homely ceiling were saying together, "We offer up to you, O God, everything we have: nothing. We are empty bowls. Fill us." As my children and I closed with the double "Amen," the whispering stilled. For just a moment, my shame was swallowed up in that worshipful quiet. For just a moment, I forgot myself–though the tremors had their strangle-hold on me–and bravely raised my shaking, empty hands. "I am an empty bowl. Fill me."

When we arrived home, moisture thickened the air. Snow, dirty and hard, still covered the ground but the day was warmer and more welcoming than those dreary February days now past. I wanted to sit in it. I wanted to be alone, to tremble in solitude.

I gestured to one of my daughters, asking with slow effort that a chair be taken into the backyard. She gladly took the closest one, a simple red dining room chair we had bought at a garage sale years earlier. She set it out in the shallow snow, a ways from the house. Then she returned to guide me out the door like an invalid, walking step by slow step with me until we were at the chair. She made sure I was securely seated before returning to the house and leaving me to my silent mental staggering.

I sat down and let bewilderment cover me like a suffocating sheet. I stopped fighting the darkness and vast wilderness around me. I stopped hiding from frailty because I couldn't do it anymore. Nothing glorious or revelatory happened. One day I just realized I had nothing left with which to fight. Like a moose stuck waist deep in the snow, I was helpless. How easily we forget how much mental strength is required to argue, to complain, to kick against God.

Although I had stopped fighting, the built up pressure in my mind and soul was palpable. The questions of identity burned inside me, a physical weight I could no longer carry.

Who was I?

Why was I?

Why such grief?

What to do? What to do? What to do? I wanted so badly to have something I could do. But I had no strength. I could not hold more than three words together at a time. Every time I tried to string together an extended thought, the words slipped off my mental tracks like a train disappearing over the cliff. I felt again the islanding effects of grief.

Suffering is personal. Although a community, a family, an entire people group might face the same loss, each member must taste the wormwood on his own tongue. The bitterness is individualized, tailored for each of us. A mystery.

This bitterness I was tasting prompted so many feelings: dread, apathy, anger. So many concerns rose inside me. For two months I had dragged my little red wagon loaded with existential questions right into God's inner chamber where I flung them at his feet. One by one I pulled them out and raged at God. I pounded my fist. I kicked the questions across the floor. I demanded an answer. And I received one, day after day, after day, after day, but not in words. I received it in the small pressure of a divine finger in my mind. Tremors.

How much longer?

Why such grief?

Lord, hear my prayer!

But that day, sitting alone in the chair, I had no

strength to compose elaborate cries. Sapped. Sagging in body and mind, I meekly uttered three words: God. Help. Me.

I said them over and over and over in my mind.

God. Help. Me.

God. Help. Me.

God. Help. Me.

Nothing noble. Nothing complex. Nothing astute. Nothing but me and my need stated frankly and simply. I have since wondered if, perhaps, this prayer is the most elemental of all prayers. Perhaps this is the most indispensable form of any petition. It communicates the essential nature of our human condition: we are destitute. Every other prayer that rises from our hearts, certainly mine, takes some form of this one.

So I prayed, for once unencumbered by false motives. Neither vanity nor greed pissed in the well of my intentions. Nothing but me, naked, before God. And I was empty. Not simply an empty vessel, but broken and empty.

God. Help. Me.

"Lord, my heart is not haughty, nor my eyes lofty. Neither do I concern myself with great matters, nor with things too profound for me. Surely I have calmed and quieted my soul."[1]

With quiet all around, with my head bobbing and my hands limp on my lap, I pleaded most childishly: God. Help. Me.

---

1   Psalm 131:1-2

Then, everything around me changed.

Snow. So uncommon that late in the year, snow began to fall around me. Massive flakes drifted down in slow motion—unhurried, without a care in the world. Within moments, a fresh blanket covered all the crusty old snow around my feet.

My cry for help continued, muffled now by the complete stillness which accompanies fresh snowfall. God. Help. Me.

Like Jonah,
"I cried out to The Lord because of my affliction,
And he answered me.
Out of the belly of Sheol I cried,
And you heard my voice.
For you cast me into the deep,
Into the heart of the seas,
And the floods surrounded me;
All your billows and your waves passed over me...
The waters surrounded me, even to my soul;
The deep closed around me;
Weeds were wrapped around my head.
I went down to the moorings of the mountains;
The earth with its bars closed behind me forever;
Yet you have brought up my life from the pit,

O Lord, my God."[2]

I wept. No call for help—just quiet weeping. The snow, like manna, piled around my feet. Manna settled on my head and caressed the tip of my nose. Manna, soft and clean, melted on my outstretched tongue. And I felt something I don't believe I can explain in words: the presence of God. He was with me and there was weight to him. His tangible presence banished panic from my mind, leaving only peace.

Now I know that God is always present. I've known that since I was a little boy. But I do not think we feel his presence very often. I certainly had not until that moment. Perhaps I am too spiritually blind or perhaps God chooses to make his presence known only at particular times. Whatever the case, with the tremors in full force and all my hopes for health, control, and strength dashed, I suddenly felt peace. Unexplainably. Surprisingly. God was with me, fulfilling his word: "Listen to me, O house of Jacob, and all the remnant of the house of Israel...even to gray hairs I will carry you! I have made, and I will bear; even I will carry, and will deliver you."[3]

I had chased peace my whole life.

I found it in my brokenness.

I found it by sitting still.

---

2   Jonah 2:1b-6

3   Isaiah 46:3-4

*"I am like a gull
lost between heaven and earth."*

Tu Fu
from "Night Thoughts"

CHAPTER 7

No One Left But God

Although my health collapse occurred nearly overnight, my recovery took much longer. Many weeks passed before I regained enough mental stamina to teach again. Even then, my mind limped from day to day, snatching at whatever remnants of past knowledge it could find. The tremors would come and go randomly and my train of thought would suddenly disappear, but my students and I grew accustomed to both.

Once again, humor danced onto the stage of my bewilderment and grief. One day as I bobbed rather violently, a student announced to the class, "Hey, everyone, today's a good day! We can say whatever we want and we won't ever be wrong!" Sure enough, no matter how I tried, I nodded through the entire day. And we laughed, even me, sincerely and happily, but yet, I still ached in my soul.

Nonetheless, after that day of sitting and praying in the falling snow, something inside my soul changed. I had tasted weakness in all its sweetness and my heart's petty demands were vanquished. Like Jacob, I now limped. But I was not destroyed. Only in my defeat did I find joy. With my back pressed against the ground of failure and frailty, something completely unexpected happened: I tasted peace, peace that passes all understanding. All along, he was really drawing me up and out into the mystery of his presence where I was less and less and he was all my sufficiency.

And God fulfilled his promise: "The poor and needy seek water, but there is none, their tongues fail for thirst. I, The Lord, will hear them; I, the God of Israel, will not forsake them. I will open rivers in desolate heights, and fountains in the midst of the valleys; I will make the wilderness a pool of water, and the dry land springs of water."[1] I was the poor and needy. I was the one wandering in the wilderness, but Christ came and gave himself to me. He, the living water, opened himself to me and became a river in desolate heights.

One day, between classes, my seventh-grade daughter approached my desk. I was pounding away at the computer, fixed on my long to-do list, only mildly aware of the tremors that coursed through my head. Though they were not visible that day, I felt them. She took my head in her hands and leaned her forehead against my own. With no one else in the

---

1   Isaiah 41:17-18

room, she maintained her embrace for a full minute.

"This is weird," I thought, chalking her actions up to those odd and unpredictable adolescent years. But I let her hold me and when she backed away, still grasping my head in her hands, she looked me in the eyes and said quietly, tenderly, "You have tremors today, don't you? I'll pray for you." Her smile broke over me like sudden sunshine onto my foggy downs, and then I knew she had pressed her head against mine to feel the tremors. She had invited herself into my suffering so she could empathize with me, walk with me, and speak to God on my behalf.

Many such moments, unexpected cups of light, made my heart weep for joy and glimpse the sun again. Each moment reminded me that my weakness, my perceived failure, was bringing about a new birth not only in me, but in those around me. Under the strain of their father's pain, my children learned how to look to God for help. They learned to rely upon him and to extend his grace into their father's life.

God used the long night of my suffering to dispel the darkness in my heart. He scattered my night like a boy rushing a murder of crows. Although I still suffer from periodic minor tremors to this day, the tenor of my soul has changed. Before, frenetic energy characterized me. Like a Formula One race-car driver, I believed that the harder and faster I went, the better life would be. A year after my first collapse in the snow, however, I consciously decided to walk slower than those around me. Tremors had forced the issue, but now my pace was more deliberate, more steady, even on my good days. On my bad days, when my face went limp and my tongue thickened in my mouth, I remembered the One who made me and I sat quietly with him.

Everything I had thought I was or needed had vanished, but I had found peace. In God's timing, certainly not my own, I had discovered what I wanted all along. Something in me had asked the decisive question: "What have I to do anymore with idols?" God heard my cry and responded : "I have heard and observed [you]. I am like a green cypress tree; your fruit is found in me."[2]

Though The Lord has graciously given me this taste of my deep need, my steps toward spiritual dependence are still halting. The next time I find myself in the wilderness, however, I will not wait in a small red chair for a moment in the snow to force dependence upon me. I will seek dependency out, prayerfully nudging my soul into God's presence. I will ask God to say to me what he has brought me into the desert to say.

I have started praying more intentionally. Each morning, I begin with these words: "Lord, as you will, and as you

---

2   Hosea 14:8

know, have mercy." I read Psalm 51 often. "O purify me, then I shall be clean!" and "Do not cast me away from your presence." At bedtime my prayers begin: "Speak, therefore, Lord, for your servant listens. You have the words of eternal life. Speak to me for the comfort of my soul and for the amendment of my life, for your praise, your glory, and your everlasting honor."[3]

The Scriptures have become more vivid to me, more charged with urgency and longing. I see more clearly God's unquenchable desire for his people. From Genesis to Revelation, I see him—the main character of the story—pressing into the story. From Adam, the judges, the prophets, and the apostles I hear our halting thirst for him. Like Simon, Andrew, James, and John, I hear the voice of my master, cast my net down, and follow him.

When the fever of self-reliance increases again, and it does sometimes, I remember being alone and destitute in the snow. I remember the peace I had in that moment and it helps the fever subside. I am learning slowly to see life as God sees it. God is giving me new eyes.

***

After serving in Kenya for nearly six years, my dad bought a home on a small river when we moved stateside. It

3   Thomas A Kempis, *The Imitation of Christ*

was the same river whose undercurrents swept me under the log when I was a teenager. My friends and I debated about whether it should be called a creek or a river. It was a moody tributary, lofty and high-spirited during the spring melt off but crestfallen, mumbling, and melancholy during late summer.

In the early mornings, as the mist sagged and brooded over the waters, I often saw the natural inhabitants awakening to the day. The stately deer, fluid and agile, inspired me by the ease with which they hurdled the high fences while raccoons appeared out of nowhere, slipping in and out of the mist. Raccoons seemed to stoop beneath large invisible packs. They skirted the bank of the river and forded the waters like derelicts: furtive, quick-tempered, and lonely.

I spent much of the summer there wandering up and down the river with a fishing pole and a stringer looped over my shoulder, or floating down the river on inner-tubes with my siblings. One summer day, when I was thirteen, my younger brother and I decided to float it as was our custom. We sprawled on tubes, the bright sun winking on the rippling water as we pressed our faces against the water's surface, following the ribbed floor of the riverbed: two boys savoring a summer day.

As we rounded a slow turn in the river, I heard dark laughter coming from the hill and looked up to see bare-chested high schoolers with sinister intent in their eyes. They were strangers to me and I wished they would go away, but it became apparent that taunting us was the temporary amusement to defer their boredom. They began calling us foul names and chucking rocks in our direction.

Their aim lacked precision and I let them know it. My words provoked nothing but rage. The boys stepped out of the underbrush, into the river, and trudged heavily toward us. Up close, their size surprised me. "What did you say?" muttered one. He menaced over me as I remained prone on the inner tube.

Pushing fights were common in school. Naive to high school conflict and, therefore, unafraid, I responded, "You heard me," with frank disregard.

He balled up his hand into a fist and sank it deep into my eye socket. The force behind his punch lifted me off the inner tube. I fell back on the tube and clutched its side. The world spun and grew dim. As the windows of my world darkened, I saw the strangers plowing through the water with high steps. My assaulter cradled his hand while the other comforted him in his pain.

I mustered all my will to keep from succumbing to darkness. "Lead me to the bridge, Nate," I whispered to my brother.

He led me three hundred yards downstream to the bridge. I held the tube like I held my consciousness: desperately, afraid of slipping into the river and sinking to the stones below. My little brother lodged me between boulders beneath the bridge.

"Run home and get Mom," I whispered and then I focused on a small point in my brain while the walls closed in. I heard my brother's bare feet slapping the stones as he scrambled up to the main road.

Maybe I slept, maybe I didn't. The mile and half of hot asphalt must have blistered my brother's little feet. I never asked. I only remember the long wait, the closing walls, and then the quiet call of my mother as she inched down the gravel and river rock to where I was lodged.

We made it home. I'm not sure how.

One week later, my head still hurt severely. As the swelling decreased, I found my vision shambled. I saw double. I could look straight ahead and still see the objects directly to my left as if they were right in front of me. After Dad tested my vision, he recognized a major problem and took me to the hospital immediately.

I remember arriving at the hospital that night; they slid me into a doughnut-shaped machine. A storm outside made the scanning process even longer. Lightning cut the power twice, forcing emergency generators to kick in. Each time the power shut down, we had to start the test over.

They tried to explain the results to me in kid-friendly language. The moment that the fist struck my eye, the bones in my face cracked and opened. In that instant, the muscles in my eye jolted and lodged in the fissure. When the facial bone retracted, it trapped the ligaments, inducing the double vision and pain. The folks in lab coats called it a blowout fracture. All I knew was that everything I looked at was skewed, dizzied, and doubled.

To repair the damage, the doctor proposed a procedure rarely done with any effect at the time. The doctor said he had performed that particular surgery only twice before. Neither patient had regained full sight. The situation demanded prayer.

A flash notice went out to everyone I knew and to people I didn't know. People rose in the middle of the night to pray for me before and after the doctor made an incision among the folds of skin beneath my eye. He peeled back the skin and separated the plates of my facial bone so that he could release the trapped muscles. Then he stitched me back together. Then we waited.

I wore a patch of bandages over my eye for several days afterward: light was harmful and healing was at a fragile point of flux. When they removed the bandages, I squinted against the bright light and saw only a fuzzy world. Within only a few weeks of the surgery, however, my eyesight was fully restored. We, including the doctor, could not explain it except by way of miracle.

I needed a miracle then to save me from possible blindness and I needed a miracle later in life to save me from spiritual blindness. It came in the form of suffering and by it I was learning to see.

***

Sometime before that day when I sat in a red chair in the falling snow, I had a dream. In my dream, I felt myself pulled by each hand in two opposing directions. My beloved wife pulled on one hand. My children pulled on her. Behind them, my parents and siblings. The line seemed to grow to include peers and students and church family and basketball team. Off in the distance stood a great and towering city filled with people whom I loved.

I felt someone pulling my other arm with a dynamically overwhelming force. I knew my surrender to that presence was only a matter of when, never a matter of if. I knew with unparalleled certainty that my wife and family's grip would fail and that the city of loved ones would fall away in its entirety. The feeling of inevitability terrified me. I turned my head to see who, or what, pulled on me with such uncontestable vitality. I saw God, or I knew that I had seen him. I saw neither his face nor his body, but it felt as though I had seen both. The mystery swallowed me. All the terror and perplexity of my soul were not eased by that glorious vision of divinity. It amplified them, devoured by the pervasive, comprehensive, and incomprehensible presence of God.

In that moment, I was the happiest I have ever been in my life, about to burst from joy, and, yet, also terrified, brittle like a china cup falling to the ground. In that moment, I knew what it was to worship the wellspring of all my joys with fear and trembling. In that moment, I knew what it was to simultaneously fear God and call him "Abba." I knew that I was unmade, facing my only dread, my deepest longing.

I had been panting as a deer longing for water. In that moment, I knew where water could be found. It could be found in the desert, in bewilderment, in terror, in suffering and in the presence of God. He did not leave me alone in the suffering nor did he leave me parched. He kept his promise to "make the wilderness a pool of water, and the dry land springs of water."[4] That dream of God pulling me gave new color to my present life.

Oh, this was joy inexpressible.

---

4   Isaiah 41:19

So, I will no longer need to be dragged into the country called Suffering. I hope not to kick against the one leading me into the wilderness. He is good, after all, intently drawing me to himself just as he did to Israel: "Now listen, I will woo her, I will go with her into the wilderness."[5]

He led me also into a lightless wilderness where I called in anguish, "Surely the darkness has fallen upon me!" But even the night became light about me for the night shone as the day. Indeed, the darkness and the light are both alike to God.[6]

**

I am easily frightened by the power of waves to capsize a boat. My friends who have fished the Alaskan waters for salmon are not so easily unsettled. They tell stories that really seem unbelievable. I know they have been terrified before and there is no doubt that any storm that worried them would doubtlessly unhinge me. Mark 4:35-41 recounts a storm so ferocious that it unhinged even veteran sailors.

Its sudden onset and majestic waves threatened not just to capsize their boat, but to smash it altogether. Spent at the end of his day, Jesus slept soundly despite the angry waters

5   Hosea 2:14 NEBV
6   Psalm 139:11-12

and the screaming men. When the disciples scrambled along the slippery deck to him, perhaps as a last resort, their cry for help sounded very much like my own during my health collapse: "Teacher, do you not care that we are perishing?"

We flounder here.

God! Help! Me!

He answered, "Peace. Be still."

The instantaneous calm created a vacuum where chaos and frantic activity once had reigned. What filled that vacuum was dread, horror, a new and boundless panic in the soul. "Who can this be?" they whispered furtively.

They wanted external peace and they got it, but it cost them the loss of their self-reliance. They had been powerless against the storm's appetite, but they discovered an entirely new level of personal powerlessness when peace was restored. What a terrifying realization to recognize that they were alone in a boat with the almighty God and no one could come to rescue them. Where could they hide from his omnipotence? They felt far more than respect for Christ; the Scripture says that "they feared exceedingly." They must have felt naked, small, fragile, deeply vulnerable in that expansive silence.

I certainly did. I was alone with God in my rickety boat of spiritual and mental confusion and could hide nowhere. After that day in the snow, when the tremors hit unexpectedly, I was terrified, as the sailors were, but now unafraid. To be terrified and yet unafraid seems a great paradox of worship, but when one has tasted it, the notion of an eternity spent terrifyingly unafraid like that is remarkably appetizing.

Come, O Lord, keep our feet upon pilgrims' ways and "lead blind men on their way and guide them by paths they do not know."[7] Guide us, O Lord, for you have promised to "turn darkness into light before them and straighten their twisting roads."[8] Your love is intrusive and insistent upon the pursuit of whom you desire. You will make yourself known, here or in the here-after, and you will draw us to yourself by whatever means necessary. All this you will do and you will leave nothing undone.

Yea, Lord, hasten the day! "And it will be said in that day: behold this is our God; we have waited for him, and he will save us. This is The Lord; we have waited for him; we will be glad and rejoice in his salvation."[9] Give us grace to follow you up from this misty lowland. We have wandered blindly far too long, but we will wander no longer.

---

7   Isaiah 42:16

8   Isaiah 42:16a NEBV

9   Isaiah 25:9

A Small Cup of Light

"I lean on a song.
I follow a story."

Li-Young Lee
from "Build by Flying"

CHAPTER 8

The Fullness Of My Cry

Some say that despair is the only viable response to suffering.
They say that suffering is proof that the world drifts rudderless,
turning as with serious purpose before stupid winds. Along
with Macbeth, they declaim this life as "a tale told by an idiot,
full of sound and fury, signifying nothing."

At one time I languished in despair; my eyes would
not close to my suffering; I lay awake like a dove alone on the
housetop.[1] At one time I said, "The darkness has come and
God has forsaken me." I did not recognize at that time that
my soul had drifted from God. The unchanging God remained
fixed at the still point of the turning wheel while I slipped
to the chaotic rim. It took God's imposed darkness to purge
the wayward drift from my soul and correct the course of my
desires.

---

1   Psalm 102:7

That was not God's only purpose in leading me into the wilderness. He is not simply a teacher or a potter, intent on changing me. God primarily wants me to desire nothing more than to be in his presence. He desires Mary's heart more than Martha's and mine was a Martha's heart. I desired distraction, interruption, and business more than I desired a contemplative walk with God in the desert.

Meister Eckhart (c. 1260-1328) once wrote, "What one grows to know and comes to love and remember, his soul follows after...If the soul were to know the goodness of God, as it is and without interruption, it would never turn away..."[2] Without interruption. But mine is a love interrupted, and so I often turn away. My spiritual Golem will not go quietly, repeatedly digging its way out of the shallow grave I have dug for it. How I have longed for the peace I felt while sitting on that red chair in the snow. How I have wished I could retrieve it some other way than through the tremors that periodically visit. Perhaps someday I will learn a way, but for now I can only remember, piecing together the place and the feelings now corroded by time.

This book tells the story of a time when God pulled me into the darkness, a darkness which scared me witless, to be alone with him. I could not escape and I learned, though grad-

---

2   Meister Eckhart, "Sermon on the Eternal Birth"

ually, that I did not actually want to escape. Since that time, my life has busied with distractions, but I have been alone with Christ. I have seen a glimpse of my real state, the one I rarely see: the truth that I have always been and will always be alone in this broken boat with him. He is the one who has delivered me from a life of death.

***

I remember the smell of the small missionary hospital in Lugulu more than I remember almost anything else about it. A mixture of body odor, Betadine, and cleaning solvents, represented the smell of disease to my childhood imagination. I learned early how to breathe through my mouth in order to dampen the scent.

My familiarity with the hospital mirrored my familiarity with my own home and with the wide Kenyan countryside that sloped toward Uganda. I played Legos with the children who sat by their parents' beds and with the children who lay so unnaturally still behind curtains of their own. When I wasn't playing with the children, I captured enormous beetles in the hospital hallways to bolster my bug collection and carried myself with all the ease of the doctor's son.

Although I was on a first name basis with the guards, I had very little idea what went on at the hospital in terms of official business. I did not know, for example, that around 1,200 infants were delivered there each year.

My father was no obstetrician. His entire medical training included only five deliveries and no experience with complications. He had studied infectious diseases and the space on his medical bookshelf dedicated to other diseases was slim. I'm sure that Dad had a how-to book on baby delivery somewhere on those shelves because I remember it (Seeing the black and white photos in that book made me foreswear an obstetric career). He also had James Herriot's veterinary stories: *All Creatures Great and Small* and *All Things Bright and Beautiful.* These books served as his most valuable obstetric manuals.

***

If only the women knew that he was studying James Herriot as pre-birth preparation—but they didn't. Nobody did. Dad tried to keep it that way. The midwives at the hospital were old pros and only needed my dad to assist when a problem arose. He would have preferred their roles reversed. When he tried to assure them that they knew more about how to handle a baby crisis than he did, they would not believe him. He was, after all, Bwana Mrefu (The Tall One). He was the lone doctor at the 110-bed, rural hospital, and great authority was granted to his position, whether he felt qualified or not.

Without anesthesia or anesthesiologist, and having only a makeshift surgery room with no sterilization, Dad refused to perform C-sections. He was restricted to hand and forceps deliveries accompanied by James Herriot's narrative voice in the back of his head. Breaches, shoulder dystocia, nuchal cord–they all had to be navigated by a man who felt more at home with skin diseases than with babies.

One day, the worst of all possible complications was brought to his attention: a laboring mother had carried a dead fetus within her. She had traveled a great distance to reach the hospital, walking the entire way, and the pain of the long journey on foot was compounded by her dead baby. The grave nurses, the distressed mother, and the entire hospital ward anticipated the birth of death into the world.

When my Dad arrived, his heart sat heavily in his chest, and he was bewildered as to how he might comfort this mother in her pain. In one last-ditch effort, he listened with a trumpet-like instrument for a heartbeat within her womb. Nothing. Then the situation suddenly degenerated even further. He realized the dead baby was out of position, unable to come out of its mother. Dad faced the possibility of losing not only the baby, but the mother as well, unless he found a way to remove the fetus.

No heartbeat. No life.

Bwana Mrefu stooped down and felt around inside the woman's uterus between contractions to discover why the baby would not come out. He found the baby in a transverse lie, its chest pressed down across the birth canal and its body arched in a violent u-shape. Its arm and hand extended out so pulling it out by the arm would break its little body.

Each contraction clamped harder on my dad's arm, now up past his elbow, as he searched with his finger to find a body part he could grab and move. What effort, both by mother and doctor, for a dead baby. He felt the urge to rip the child from the womb just to save the mother, but something in his mind told him to deliver the child correctly: be the physician and do things right.

Dead baby or no dead baby, he did things right. He stretched his fingers until he found the knobby point above the child's hip and could reposition the baby into a breach position: butt downward. Do it right. As the baby's rump came out, he reached in and swept one arm down across the face and chest so that the baby's arm would not break when squeezed out, then he found the other arm and did the same. Carefully, so carefully.

The contractions did their work and violently pressed the baby out: a baby without breath, silent, still. Dad removed his arm and encouraged the grieving mother to push.

Push for what?

Why?

She was in anguish of body and heart, birthing her grief. Slowly, gradually, the baby entered the waiting world. Butt first, then legs. Bwana Mrefu held it up by its tiny legs and reached for its head when the lifeless baby, the upside down baby, the baby with no heartbeat, gasped and woke the world from its grief with a wail that was not soon forgotten.

Prepared to receive a dead baby, no one had prepared the suction tube to clear the infant's mouth of mucus. Dad called excitedly for help and a flurry of happy activity erupted. The aftershocks of that infant's cry rippled across the entire ward, and joy, slow in coming, cautious like a doe, broke into exultation and triumph. Joy gamboled like a young deer across the open fields of their imaginations. Tears and laughter, relief and amazement, all commingled in one beautiful moment.

***

Like that infant, my health collapse cramped my soul, pressing me down. Like that infant, I was alive, but barely. Who would deliver me? What an awful, stranded, impotent position. In the grip of tremors and mental confusion, I could only wait like the psalmist: "I wait for the Lord, my soul doth wait, and in his word do I hope."[3] I could only confirm with the prophet, "It is good that one should hope and wait quietly for the salvation of the Lord."[4] Or agree with the afflicted Job, "All the days of my hard service I will wait, till my change comes."[5]

Ezekiel proclaimed, "You shall be desolate, then you shall know that I am The Lord."[6] God asserts that desolation precedes a deeper knowledge of him. He will strip us of any pretense of self-sufficiency, of any ability to conjure our own salvation. This spiritual desolation takes many forms and its path is non-linear. It is also hard to measure. For these reasons, the process from pain to resolution is messy, made all the messier when I tried to evade it. God did not give me suffering so that I might only look beyond it to some happy vale of future delight. He gave me suffering as a gift to be held in the present moment, just as he has given me happiness as a gift of the here and now.

Like Augustine who agonized with God, I face the intimate and terrifying truth of God's intentions. Like Augustine I say to God, "You have compassion on our dust and ashes...By

3   Psalm 130:5 KJV

4   Lamentations 3:26

5   Job 14:14

6   Ezekial 35:4

the secret hand of your healing my swelling was lessened, the disordered and darkened eyesight of my mind was from day to day made whole by the stinging salve of wholesome grief."

Suffering dissolves the illusion of my own self focus. Suffering is a thrust, a nudge, away from my swollen self-intoxication which sends me stumbling into the presence of God where joy is found. The life of true freedom and wholeness is found only in the lap of God where I most dread to go and where I most want to be.

I pray haltingly, therefore, with Thomas A Kempis: "If you wish me to be in darkness, I shall bless you. And if you wish me to be in light, again I shall bless you. If you stoop down to comfort me, I shall bless you, and if you wish me to be afflicted, I shall bless you forever."[7]

My change did come, as it came for Job. God placed his finger on my body and mind. Crisis resulted, a kind of death, but my change came. Now I live a new resurrection, each day opening my eyes wider to see as God sees.

Living with debilitating tremors has taught me that all my busy activity is unnecessary for spiritual maturation. It's not so much about what I'm doing for God, but what he is doing in my life and the world at large. Accepting my human frailty liberated me from the slavery imposed by a god who demanded

---

7   Thomas A Kempis, *The Imitation of Christ*

my good deeds, a god I had imagined. When I was most frail, I could do nothing but learn to listen and learn to see what God was doing.

I have come to learn that the means to lasting change is found not by doing something differently, but seeing with new eyes. It comes by transforming the imagination. I must learn to see myself in all my nakedness, to see my vulnerability and frailty and who I really am underneath this bluster and posturing.

I am an arrow shot from a bow string.

I am a bird in flight.

I am a falling leaf.

Never at rest. For this reason, John Wesley wrote, "I have thought I am a creature of a day, passing through life as an arrow through the air. I am a spirit come from God and returning to God; just hovering over the great gulf, till a few moments hence I am no more seen.[8]" Life is brief. And though I fly like a bird, suffering will remain like a sack of stones tied to my ankles, keeping me from flying straight; indeed, without God I will continue to plummet out of the sky, whirling and flapping, beak agonizingly extended. God. Help. Me.

I found God in an unexpected place; rather, God found me. In my desert despair he gave me himself. He gave

---

8   John Wesley, *A Man With One Book*

me peace: a small cup of light.

***

My daughter can't sleep tonight. She's the same daughter who needed all those tubes to keep her breathing when she was tiny. She's older now and although we have visited the doctor and although we have given her the medicine he prescribed, she is having difficulty breathing again. It's not a cause of devastating grief, but it's an affliction for her. She doubles over in my arms, sometimes arching her back and neck to gasp for breath. I rock her slowly, sitting on the edge of the bed. What to do? What to say to her in her small desert of suffering? Shall I tell her about barking dogs at night? Or hawks at dusk? Will she hear me speak of hens' wings, warm and strong?

I smooth back her damp hair. Seeing her so small and frail reminds me of some lines from Rilke:

"Since I still don't know enough about pain,
this terrible darkness makes me small.
If it's you, though--
press down hard on me, break in
that I may know the weight of your hand,
and you, the fullness of my cry."[9]

---

9   Rainer Maria Rilke, "It Feels As Though I Make My Way"

Exhausted from the strain, my girl keeps groaning, keeps pulling in small breaths.

"Oh, darling, it's alright to cry. It's alright," I whisper. "God's with you in this place right now. Better yet, he is painting you. These are the dark paint strokes; you, the masterpiece."

Her groaning stops. She listens.

"You are God's precious girl. You're even more precious to him than you are to me. Can you believe that? He has led you here, into this painful place, so there's nothing to fear."

Her breathing quiets. I lean toward her ear and whisper, "Sit in the suffering, my skittish dove. Listen to the voice of God. What is he singing? He is not silent." I keep murmuring into her ear as she coasts into sleep's haven, "Here's a small cup of light. Take and drink." Then I pray words over her that she is too frail to speak herself and too young to know:

"I moan like a dove.
My eyes are weary with looking upward.
    O Lord, I am oppressed; be my pledge of safety!
What shall I say? For he has spoken to me,
    and he himself has done it.
I walk slowly all my years
    because of the bitterness of my soul.

O Lord, by these things men live,

and in all these is the life of my spirit."[10]

Grief swells up in my memory, a dark wave looming in my mind. I remember being pulled into the wilderness by God, the inevitable God. I remember the suburbs of my mind going dark in front of my class. I remember the moose waste-deep in snow. I remember sitting in a red chair, tremors coursing through my body, pleading, "God help me." I remember my earthly father ill-prepared to deliver that baby. And then, in a wave of gladness, I remember my Heavenly Father, the great physician competent to deliver and heal.

I gaze at my girl and remember that though he deliver us by way of wilderness, yet the Lord saves his own and answers those who call for help.[11] I remember snow, the quiet of the day wrapping itself around me, the peace that passes understanding enveloping me in my utter brokenness, and I celebrate a God who will do whatever he must to draw us near to himself.

My little girl is asleep, despite her tears, and I delicately tuck her under the covers. Smoothing her damp curls one more time, I listen to her steady breathing, kiss her, and

---

10   Isaiah 38:14-16 ESV

11   Psalm 20:6

stand in the doorway for a moment. Turning out the light, I head down the hall and climb into bed, the same place on the bed in which I once curled into the fetal position—groaning in my soul. I recall the despair, still fresh in my memory and remember my wife whispering into my ear: "Be gracious to me, O God, be gracious; for I have made thee my refuge."

Though night may again fall upon me suddenly, you, O God, will be my refuge. Though I find myself in a desert, stumbling beneath a starless sky, still, I will listen for the shy song of that small bird, Hope. I will follow it, weeping and singing.

So it is and so it will be.

Weep and sing.

Despair is not the only viable response to suffering. I offer a different one: celebration. I celebrate God in all his majesty. I celebrate frailty. I celebrate dependency, yearning, and smallness. Hatched into life beneath an opal sky, I wing my way to God. Even in the night, I rise as a dove and perch alone on the housetop. In the darkness of affliction, I will sing.

A Small Cup of Light

*"Suffering is permanent, obscure
and dark, and shares
the nature of infinity."*

William Wordsworth
from *The Borderers, Act III*

CHAPTER 9

Conclusion: Wearing Grief Well

Suffering is night, a brooding blank on the soul's staring eye. Those who have suffered deeply remember the constriction, the immobilizing fear and doubt. A million moments of laughter and pleasure in life may slip from memory, but we recall the pain with ease.

The suffering chronicled in this book happened some years ago, but the memories remain fresh. Still, it has taken a long time for me to learn a key lesson of that season: joy sometimes saddles despair's back. I learned and continue to learn that it is possible to ride despair toward God. This is a praiseful realization: love is bit and bridle, despair, the beast. To live well is to learn how to ride, how to lean into grief.

Lean into grief.

But how do we, a people so desperate for microwave solutions, embrace the mystery of a God who invites us into suffering? We want a checklist cure to our troubles, but God is less interested in solving them than he is in shaping us for eternity. As he sings the story of the world, he seems intent on weaving darkness into our individual stories, the memories of which we will always have.

***

The physical and mental losses from my health crisis continue to affect me. I still live with loss. Sometimes the tremors visit me while I drive to church on a sunny day or when I lie down to sleep. Their arrival is always a gradual, unpleasant surprise. I continue to face the limitations of a frail body and a mind that sometimes veers off its tracks.

While the suffering is certainly diminished right now, the memories remain vivid. In some ways I am a traveler who can look back on a particularly difficult part of my path from a higher vantage point. But I think that metaphor fails to account for all the pain I still carry with me. As though I made it to the other side of the trial and can now move on. At some deep place inside, we'd like to simply get through our suffering and move on, but this does not accurately picture reality.

One of my mentors lost his mother, wife, and daughter in one car accident. I asked him how he answers those who want to just get through their suffering. His response? "Ben, I've been living through broken glass for twenty-two years. You never get over grief. It's a part of you forever, and you can only learn to wear it well."

I think that's the best way to describe where I am now, years removed from the events of this book. I'm not on the other side of anything; rather, I'm still walking through this valley of tears, commonly called "life." It is a mistake to think that I can just get through my trials. We are the accumulation of our experiences and we do ourselves a disservice if we embrace only the happy parts of our story. The dark moments of our existence are also worth valuing because they are an essential part of the story that a good God is telling. They are not an accident of existence.

But all our stories, played out on a global stage, have their fair share of anguish and confusion. A season of confusion or grief falls on each of us. Some people seem saddled with a lifetime of pain. What shall we do, then, born and dying in this global triage unit? What shall we do when confronted with the reality of our suffering and the truth of a living God?

I have come slowly, limping, to the realization that I am imagined by God, tremors included. I am his precious character living out a small bit part in his epic. My tremors remain a part of that epic story. They are not the resolution. They are the in-between. In Tolkien's Middle Earth, they are the Mines of Moria and Gandalf gone. In the gospel stories, they are

Christ's disciples huddled together in a darkened room, scared and bewildered, all their hopes swallowed up by a tomb. They are Isaiah crying out, "'Look away from me, I will weep bitterly...' For it is a day of trouble and treading down and perplexity by the Lord God of hosts in the Valley of Vision—Breaking down the walls and of crying to the mountain."[1]

While I lay on the couch and quietly seethed in my anger, when I fought against the fracturing of my mind, I was simply an extension of God's story. A story characterized by pain.

His story is colored by the murder of a brother, the rape of a sister, the betrayal of a friend, the pounding of nails into flesh and bone, and the darkening of the sky. A world of what-ifs and could-have-beens, peopled by has-beens and might-have-beens. It is a world soaked in fear and drenched by the blood of a million martyrs. A world of men burned at the stake and babes slaughtered at their mother's breasts. A dark history with pain oozing into all its hidden corners.

At the center of history is a death. Christ's death, the decisive point of history. Christianity is perhaps the most morbid religion of the world. Perpetually meditating upon death with little crosses hung around their necks, Christian disciples sing their way to martyrdom.

---

1   Isaiah 22:5

Anticipating death and calling it gain, Christians are evangelists of the grotesque. The very hope of the Gospel rests directly upon our ability to imagine a world in which suffering serves as the soil from which resurrection springs.

***

I knew all this during my personal crisis. I simply did not want my martyrdom to take the form of debilitation. How I would have traded my bed-ridden anxieties for some glorious showdown with persecution. Go ahead, put a gun to my head, threaten me with needles under a naked, glaring bulb in a damp basement. Go ahead, bring out the villains. Instead, my death took the form of weakness. It all felt ignoble, a story terribly bungled.

I wanted so badly to prove myself a man, to shed my consuming frailty and return to my ambitions. All the while, God was weaving a tapestry. I could not see the tapestry because it was largely unthreaded and so I had no idea that the death I was experiencing was necessary for resurrection. Little did I know that God was not testing my faith in order to find out its quality. He didn't need to discover what he already knew.[2] I was the one who had not measured its buoyancy. I knew not its durability nor the power of its wing.

---

2   C.S. Lewis, *A Grief Observed*

How long must I learn to carry this grief in faith? How lasting is suffering's effect on the soul? Heaven promises to be a place without grief, without tears. Does that mean that I forget my story in Heaven? I don't think so.

Jesus, enthroned at the right hand of God in Heaven, has not forgotten his suffering on the cross. Hebrews 4:15 says that he sympathizes with us in our weakness—his fellowship with our trials is ongoing. And he did not mount the cross begrudgingly. The Anglo-Saxon people imagined the crucified Christ as a warrior mounting his war horse. Glad anguish. His suffering has comforted generations of Christians who shared intimately in that suffering. And their suffering is a reminder that we are not alone in our wilderness even now. We join the great cloud of witnesses and we join Christ in the wilderness of suffering. He is the firstborn of all creation who showed us the way of the cross, the way of glad anguish.

We will spend eternity remembering his suffering on our behalf and rejoicing because we will fully understand how his suffering and our suffering glorified the father. I have a hunch that we'll spend eternity remembering our own suffering also, learning how to wear it well, remembering that Christ's suffering redeemed our own, and realizing how our trials worked to glorify God, the great Story-Teller. All our singing will be prompted not by forgetfulness, but by thankfulness. We will spend eternity gripped by a deep, gut-level thankfulness; indeed, we will weep for the glad tidings of this great joy: Jesus, the Christ, came to save sinners. He is Emmanuel, "God with us." Even in the darkness, even when we are sleepless despite grief's fatigue, God is with us.

At the writing of this epilogue, I have five children. At least two of whom remember nothing of these events. My only son, the one who found me burrowing into the snow, has no ready recollection of that moment. But I know that his father's frailties, despite my efforts to hide them, have shaped him in significant and immeasurable ways.

So it is also true that my suffering is not my own. I am not the only one learning to wear this grief well. My wife is learning, too. My children and those who walked with me during this chapter of life were shaped and are still being shaped by those events.

Here we are, then, at the end of our proverbial rope, a rope woven by Christ, and here, God finds us. Or, rather, we finally see him; he was here all along. This is the gospel of good news and precisely why Christ ran to sinners, not those who thought themselves righteous. Only the sick and broken, those at the end of their resources, know that they need help. He calls us up and out into a mystery where we are emptied. He presses in on us until we sit still in the dark and listen to his quiet voice. There, in the quiet brokenness, Christ meets us as God has always met his people.

***

When I consider how God loves to encounter his characters during their deepest need, I remember Hagar wandering in the wilderness by the spring on the way to Shur.[3] Abused and afraid for her life, Hagar fled, finding the wilderness and the possibility of rape or death more tolerable than the prospect of remaining under Sarai's authority.

Weary and half-starved, she sat by the spring alone, pregnant, and terrified. Then, just when her story appeared dead, purposeless, the author entered his own story. In the first recorded Christophany, the pre-incarnate visitation of the Word, the Logos, the one with all authority and power, the one who holds all things together, the Son of the living God, approached her in her loneliness.

Hagar wanted out of her suffering. Hagar wanted to get to the other side of her pain. Hagar was bewildered in the wasteland when the Living Water appeared to her. I'm sure Hagar wanted words of comfort like we would, something to encourage her sagging soul. Perhaps she wanted answers, something solid and objective and measurable. We might

---

3   Genesis 16

expect Christ's words at that moment to take the form of a declarative sentence like, "I have come to comfort you." Or a simple command, "Don't cry." Instead, Christ interrogated her. "Where have you come from and where are you going?" he asked. His question forced her to confront herself, to assess her current imagination, to hold up the story she saw herself in against the story he was actually telling.

Like Hagar, I would choose to flee my troubles, but Christ asks me, "Where have you come from and where are you going?"[4] Like Hagar, I only know what I am fleeing. I remain unable to make sense of God's providence, authority, love, or promises in the snapshot of my trial. Only in the larger story do these things become clear. So I sit in the sand, beneath the starless sky, and wait for my change to come.[5]

Christ leads us into the wilderness of suffering to engage us there. When he meets us in the wilderness, he is manna, he is water from a broken rock. But he is also the one who wants us to potently feel our lack so that we cling to him. The Apostle Paul expressed as much when he wrote, we are "sorrowful, yet always rejoicing."[6] God is the one who leads us into the desert and who makes us feel exposed and frail there. He is

---

4   Genesis 16:8

5   Job 14:14

6   II Cor. 6:10

the one who turns the wilderness into a womb from which his children are born into gladness. And, like Hagar, we cry, "You are the God who sees."[7]

My words inadequately communicate the depth and breadth and height of the Father's love for his children. The message of this chapter, this book, and my life is simply this: God gets all the glory. His name is elevated above all men, all circumstances, all fear, all loneliness, all suffering. God's love for his people is all that matters, and it is his love that prompts us to sing in the darkness and wear our grief well.

***

When I was about nine years old, my Dad took me on a road trip across the Kenyan border into Uganda, at that time, a war-torn country, seething in the daylight and raging at night. I remember sleeping on the floor of an apartment in one of Uganda's major cities and hearing popcorn popping somewhere.

"Dad, why is someone popping popcorn in the middle of the night?" I asked.

"That's not popcorn, Son." He hesitated. "That's gunfire." He probably felt my body tighten in the darkness. "It sounds like popcorn because it's so far away. Don't worry, we're

7   Genesis 16:13

safe." I don't know if he slept that night. I did, albeit, fitfully.

We drove into the countryside the next afternoon. Our friend, a refugee from the brutal Idi Amin regime, wanted us to see a homemade xylophone. Driving through miles of darkening banana plantations, I imagined guerrilla fighters, crouched in the shadows with automatic rifles hoisted over their shoulders and machetes clinched in their teeth. I questioned the value of flirting with death just to see a homemade xylophone. The road narrowed until it became impassable, so we climbed out and walked the rest of the way in darkness, my terror growing with every step.

We arrived late in the evening at a home tucked in the middle of a banana plantation. Like many of the families I knew as a boy, four generations, extended family, lived together under a few roofs. They served us supper, then ushered us outside under the spangled Milky Way.

We stood together in the quiet night in an open space of some fifty feet of packed clay. I knew that miles of banana trees lay beyond the light of the torches, possible shelter to an army of blood-thirsty warriors. Or so said my imagination. Fear nearly paralyzed me, but the Christian family moved to sing as Christian families do.

In the open space, they had built a massive xylophone, some fifteen feet long, large enough for several people to play on it at one time. A large hole dug in the clay, three feet deep and five feet wide, extended under a portion of the instrument. Forming its sides, two long banana tree trunks ran parallel to one another. Notches in both trunks held hand-carved boards that bridged between them as the bars of the xylophone.

While I stood there imagining horrid faces in the surrounding shadows, one young man took up some homemade mallets, strode to the xylophone and began to play a simple, rhythmic melody at one end, the end farthest from the heavier bars. He played it repeatedly for a minute and then an older man started to play a different set of notes, a rhythmic improvisation, at the other end. He pounded the bars that laid over the dugout hole, and their deep, bull sound resounded farther into the sky as a result.

Then a third man joined the fun, followed by another man. Four men whaling on wood, playing their hearts out in the darkness. The family started clapping, some carrying the firm beat while others alternated, clapping on the off-beat. Then someone started singing and the rest joined. While they sang and played joyfully, I sat terrified. The ruckus would surely wake the warriors from their slumbers. I imagined the banana plantation swarming with fighters all moving stealthily toward this small space under the stars.

Despite my fears, the children clapped and sang, their

glad faces shining under the flickering torch-light. They were singing in a tongue I could not understand, but their vibrant and brilliant song filled the darkness. The music rose into the sky, it reverberated off the trees, and I found myself suddenly, unexpectedly swept up on a wave of gladness.

And then I found myself clapping with them, at first shyly and then fervently, hand-hurting claps on the off-beat. I stopped looking furtively into the darkness behind and around me. Gazing into all of those shining faces, I felt my spirit buoyed by the banging xylophone and loud, generational voices. I lost track of time. I didn't forget the shadows nor did I forget the warriors who may or may not have lurked amongst them. But their possible presence paled in comparison with the joy I felt in my heart.

I realize now how much fear I brought to that gathering those many years ago in Uganda. I realize now that they had something I lacked and they gave it to me as a gift, inviting me into their joy. I remember feeling so naked and exposed, like a field mouse under the night sky. I remember my foreboding and the sudden joy that swept me up on a wave of song. It took a singing Ugandan family to teach me this lesson, but we need not travel to some remote part of the war-ripped world to find the gift of joy, the gift of hope, the gift of singing in the dark. We can have it even here, even now. We can offer it to each other, singing strong songs with our faces shining in the night.

Rejoice with me. In this valley of tears, this valley of the shadow of death, God has given us songs to sing. We are singing pilgrims, so sing with all your heart. God is our song. When we sing in the darkness, our songs reverberate back to us and make us glad.

May this book be a small cup of light for you, dear friend. Take and drink. Lift up weary hands and frightened face to God. Lean into his story. Even in the darkness, he is there. He is the one beside you, singing you. Remember. And this is my prayer: May you find his light in your darkness, his life in your death, his joy in your sorrow. Forever and ever.

Amen.

A Conversation With The Author

Why did you choose the title, A Small Cup of Light?

The title comes from a poem, titled "Tuesday, June 4, 1991," by Billy Collins, in which he personifies early morning as a peasant woman who offers him a handful of birdsong and a small cup of light. I thought that was a beautiful picture of what God did during my suffering. He offered me small cups of light, small tastes of hope. Those small tastes of light really amplified my longing for him, very much like the psalmist who wrote, "My soul thirsts for God, for the living God" (Psalm 42:2). Now I've written a book that I hope will serve as a small cup of light for those living with suffering.

Why did you write the book?

I wrote this book for two reasons: first, to process my health collapse. Writing this book afforded me the opportunity to deal with a significant event in my life. I was able to retrace my steps through that suffering and listen a second time to what the Holy Spirit was saying. I also wrote this book because I think suffering is one of the most important subjects we can tackle, for our own sake at the very least. What could be more urgent or more relevant than suffering?

There are many kinds of suffering. I'm thinking of the rape victim and others who have suffered incredible brutality. What would you say to someone who has suffered tremendous abuse or witnessed atrocities?

I'd want to tell them that I thought a lot about them while I wrote this book. In fact, I had a hard time really confronting my own suffering because it paled in comparison to the atrocious pain and grief that others experience. Thankfully, a dear friend pulled the rug out from under that argument when he said, "Ben, until you take your own pain seriously, you'll never hear what God is trying to tell you in it. Stop avoiding God by dismissing your particular story."

Those were wise words that I haven't forgotten. There's

no doubt that many, many others have suffered far more than I have, but I can only climb into the mystery and brokenness of *my* pain. It's much harder to successfully climb into other people's pain and I will have zero success, zero empathy, until I've come to terms with mine. Who knows what God has in store for my life, what kinds of pain I'll encounter? But there are certain reliable promises God has given us to hold on to as we walk through this valley of tears. Writing this book helped me not only recognize those promises, but also claim them as my own.

What are some of those promises that sufferers need?

Well, God has promised that he is good (Mark 10:18, Psalm 145:9, Psalm 107:1) and that he is intimately in charge of history (Daniel 4:35, Proverbs 19:21, Isaiah 45:6-7). It's easy to doubt both those promises when we look around, but we can still count on them because they come from a reliable God (II Cor. 1:20). Scripture makes it clear that history is God's story (Psalm 119:9-91), he's obviously telling it and his telling includes the dark parts of the story. God is good and nothing falls outside his plan. Those two promises have become a great comfort to me.

Are you suggesting that we'll see the purpose for our suffering in this life?

I don't think there's any way I can guarantee that we'll see why something happened before we come face to face with our Maker. I don't think we'll see the big picture until we're on the other side. We still see through a smudged window (I Cor. 13:12) and that means we may not see our suffering redeemed on this side of heaven. Nonetheless, God is in control of all happenings and he is good.

Since God is good, isn't it true that God can't be held responsible for atrocities performed by sinful, fallen human beings? Do you agree with those who say that, "God doesn't cause calamity, but he can use it for good"?

It helps me to remember that we mortals usually wake up with a plan for the day. If that principle is true of us, how much more so for the God who made us. A God without a plan is no God at all. As A.J. Gordon wrote, "A universe without decrees would be as irrational and appalling as would be an express train driving on in the darkness without headlight or engineer, and with no certainty that the next moment it might not plunge into the abyss."

Some well-intentioned folks want to give God sovereignty only over the big events, but there really aren't any small moments because each one has its exact place in God's bigger plan. Big events are downstream from a million small moments. Control of big events requires control of little events. I believe God's plan is specific, involving the details of our lives, and our suffering is meaningless if we suggest that God isn't somehow in charge of suffering, especially brutalities.

The Bible teaches that God "works all things after the counsel of his will" (Ephesians 1:11). "All things" seems pretty all-inclusive. It includes small events and big ones. Little events like a falling sparrow (Matthew 10:29) or a rolling die (Proverbs 16:33) are under the sovereign will of God just like big events are. Persecution (Hebrews 12:4-17), birth and death (I Samuel 2:6), daily plans (James 4:15), and a king's decisions (Proverbs 21:1) are all under his control.

I'm reminded of that great calamity, the Chicago fire of 1871, which killed hundreds of people. Legend has it that it started when a cow kicked over a lantern. The impact of that fire was massive, but Amos asks a provocative question I don't think we can afford to ignore in this circumstance: "If a calamity occurs in a city has not the LORD done it?" (Amos 3:6). The New York catastrophe of September 11, 2001, even more than the Chicago fire, impacted many lives in atrocious and immeasurable ways. Still, God governs them intimately according to his good, just, and wise purposes (Isaiah 46:10). Job suffered more than most, but even while covered in boils he said, "Shall we indeed accept good from God and not accept adversity?" (Job 2:10).

It's true that our suffering is a product of sin and part of the consequences of living in a fallen world, but that truth is only one side of the coin. The other side of that coin is that God is in control. Yes, people do horrible things, myself included, and we are responsible for those actions. Yes, people are free to make wicked choices, but they aren't at liberty to make those decisions apart from God's sovereign control. We are not autonomous beings and those who keep preaching human autonomy rob us of our only hope; namely, a good God who has complete authority over all things and who comes to the aid of those who cry out to him. Suffering in every form is meaningless and hopeless unless God is in control of it.

What are three principles that helped you during suffering?

As I've already said, the first principle is that God is sovereign: my suffering does not come as a surprise to him and, in fact, it's a very important part of the story that he is telling. Another principle is that God will remove my suffering in his timing, not mine. I think it was Brother Lawrence who wrote that God will take us off of our cross when he is ready to do so and not a moment before or after. Be patient.

Another principle that took me a long time to learn was that God uses suffering to speak to us. We need to be still and listen to him in our suffering. Pray. Soak in the Scripture. And pray some more. I remember Paul's beautiful prayer for his friends where he asks God to give them both patience and faith in their suffering. He prays that God would fulfill all his good pleasure and glorify the name of Christ in them during their suffering (II Thess. 1:4 and 11). It's striking to me that he doesn't ask God to make the suffering go away. In another place, he asks that God would remove his affliction (II Cor. 12:8). When Paul makes that request, he's simply imitating Christ who asked God to remove the coming affliction when he was in the Garden, just before his crucifixion (Luke 22:42). So I'm learning to imitate Paul in both respects, to pray first for patience and faith and then to pray for healing.

Finally, I learned that suffering provokes in us a deep longing for God. Christians are fond of saying that suffering makes us better people. I don't think that's always true, but I do think that suffering amplifies the fact that this is not our home. We long for our heavenly home.

What are some lessons you carry with you after the health collapse?
Well, there are a lot of lessons I've learned. I can't say I've learned them all in a permanent way, but I'm trying to live

by them. One of the most important lessons and the one I have the hardest time implementing is to set margins in life. I have people who know me well and they keep an eye on me to make sure that I'm not over-committing. Busyness isn't a virtue and most of the activity in our lives simply distracts us from listening to God's still, small voice (I Kings 19:12). It often keeps us not only from encountering God, but from a genuine encounter with real people in real time.

I think another lesson I learned is that life is not so much about what I'm doing for God as much as it is about how I'm learning to see what God is up to in my life. I try too hard to please God by my efforts instead of letting my efforts spring naturally from a kind of thankfulness for what he has done and is doing in my life. Perhaps the hardest prayer I've learned to pray is this one: "Lord, I'm ready for you to do whatever you must to draw me close to you." It's a terrifying prayer for some reason, but it's also very liberating to vocalize.

If you were to offer one piece of advice to those walking through their own wilderness season, what would it be?

I'd tell them to imitate Job. He didn't pretend to be happy during his suffering. He didn't look for distractions from his pain. He didn't find solace in other people. Nor was he passively mute in the face of God. Job was actually very vocal with God, asking "Why?" right to God's face. I think that's the best way to deal with suffering: ask the hard questions, wrestle with what God is doing, but do it all face to face with God. That approach to suffering mirrors so many characters including the prophets and especially the Psalmist. I think any other response to suffering is not only unbiblical, it's spiritually and emotionally unhealthy.

What about those who serve sufferers? What advice would you give to those who live with and serve people who are suffering?

Eugene Peterson said, "Suffering attracts helpers, like roadkill attracts flies." So I think it's important to resist the temptation to quickly fix the problem. I'm all for medication and the aids of modern science, but, as I mentioned earlier, we tend to look for a solution first, instead of listening to God in our suffering first.

Another small piece of advice is that a person's suffering might be for you as much as for them. I think it's easy to get self-righteous and assume that someone else's suffering is God working on them, but it might very well be that their suffering is for you, not them. Maybe God is using their suffering to draw you closer to himself.

Finally, I think it's easy to grow impatient with those who suffer. I'm thinking especially of those with chronic pain or depression, or those whose lives seem to consist of one problem after another. In those cases, we just need to ask God for the grace to walk with them for the long mile. What was Christ's response to suffering? Compassion. He is now, and will remain, our model.

Finally, what's your hope for this book?

I hope this book will have a life of its own, encouraging sufferers the world over, whether in hospitals or in lonely houses. I can't be in all those places at once, comforting them as I'd like, but this book can. Most of all, I hope this book glorifies the name of Jesus who has redeemed me, given me new life, and taught me how to sing my suffering.

Acknowledgments

Herman Melville once wrote, "No man is his own sire." The same goes for a book. Many people deserve thanks, some dead and some alive, for helping deliver this book into the world. I offer my sincere thanks to all of you.

I owe special thanks, however, to Amy Kim for herding the climbing cats of my prose into marching order. Her tireless and cheerful editing and insights are (present tense) a priceless gift to me. Any remaining blunders in the book are mine.

Thanks, also, to those who read early versions and encouraged me to press on: Keith Wall, Paul Moede, Shann Ferch, Jerry Sittser, Bruce Williams, Mom and Dad, Andrea and Steve Dilley, Bill and Cherise Stutzman, George Grant, Van Lahmeyer, Lucy Nolan, David Wang, and Kenton Spratt.

Heartfelt thanks goes to Dave Hutchins, Bruce Williams, my parents, and my wife for sitting with me during the wilderness season recounted in this book and encouraging me to listen to God.

I also owe a debt of gratitude to my church family and my family at The Oaks–staff, students, and families–who walked through this season with me and who remain dear friends. Thank you for enriching my life.

Thank you to those who have helped me to see God and his story more clearly and more richly: John Piper, John Frame, Douglas Wilson, J.I. Packer, N.D. Wilson, Joost Nixon, and Stuart Bryan.

Finally, I could never adequately thank my wife who still loves me after all these years and affords me time to write. She is a faithful companion on this pilgrimage, fresh air to my heart and sunshine to my thoughts.

And, of course, thank you to Kiale, Hannah, Noah, Samantha, and Eliana for being my children and the stars in my sky. I fold my hands behind my head, smile, and watch you light the world.

A Small Cup of Light

Credits

Every effort has been made to contact all copyright holders. The publishers would be happy to rectify any omissions at the first opportunity.

Excerpt from "Tuesday, June 4, 1991" from The Art of Drowning, by Billy Collins, copyright 1995. Reprinted by permission of the University of Pittsburgh Press.

Confessions, by St. Augustine, copyright 2004 and *The Imitation of Christ*, by Thomas A Kempis, copyright 2004 by Hendrickson Publishers, Peabody, Massachusetts. Used by permission. All rights reserved.

Li-Young Lee, "Build by Flying" from Book of My Nights. Copyright © 2001 by Li-Young Lee. Reprinted with the permission of The Permissions Company, Inc., on behalf of BOA Editions, Ltd., www.boaeditions.org

Unless otherwise indicated, Scripture quotations are from The Holy Bible, New King James Version, Copyright 1982 by Thomas Nelson, Inc. Used by Permission. All rights reserved.

All NEBV references are Scripture quotations from The Holy Bible, The New English Bible, Oxford University Press 1970. All ESV references are Scripture quotations from The Holy Bible, English Standard Version, copyright 2001 by Crossway Bibles, a division of Good News Publishers. Used by permission. All rights reserved.

A Small Cup of Light